ntents

Chapter 1: Working parents and finance

Chapter 2: Family Life

Chapter 3: Teen pregnacy and fatherhood

Introduction

CHANGING FAMILIES is Volume 329 in the **ISSUES** series. The aim of the series is to offer current, diverse information about important issues in our world, from a UK perspective.

ABOUT CHANGING FAMILIES

This book explores the Modern Family and how it manages the balance between family life and work. It looks at the increasing number of full-time working mothers with young children. The book also considers what impact increasing levels of parental involvement might have on children, and the role fathers have to play in their children's everyday lives and development. It also explores teenage parenting.

OUR SOURCES

Titles in the **ISSUES** series are designed to function as educational resource books, providing a balanced overview of a specific subject.

The information in our books is comprised of facts, articles and opinions from many different sources, including:

⇨ Newspaper reports and opinion pieces

⇨ Website factsheets

⇨ Magazine and journal articles

⇨ Statistics and surveys

⇨ Government reports

⇨ Literature from special interest groups.

A NOTE ON CRITICAL EVALUATION

Because the information reprinted here is from a number of different sources, readers should bear in mind the origin of the text and whether the source is likely to have a particular bias when presenting information (or when conducting their research). It is hoped that, as you read about the many aspects of the issues explored in this book, you will critically evaluate the information presented.

It is important that you decide whether you are being presented with facts or opinions. Does the writer give a biased or unbiased report? If an opinion is being expressed, do you agree with the writer? Is there potential bias to the 'facts' or statistics behind an article?

ASSIGNMENTS

In the back of this book, you will find a selection of assignments designed to help you engage with the articles you have been reading and to explore your own opinions. Some tasks will take longer than others and there is a mixture of design, writing and research-based activities that you can complete alone or in a group.

Useful weblinks

www.acas.org.uk

www.belfasttelegraph.co.uk

www.cam.ac.uk

www.centreforsocialjustice.org.uk

www.childandfamilyblog.com

www.theconversation.com

www.era.lib.ed.ac.uk

www.ucl.ac.uk

www.huffingtonpost.co.uk

www.ibtimes.com

www.ilcuk.ork.uk

www.independent.co.uk

www.local.gov.uk

www.nhs.uk

www.telegraph.co.uk

www.theguardian.com

www.tuc.org.uk

www.visual.ons.gov.uk

www.workingfamilies.org.uk

FURTHER RESEARCH

At the end of each article we have listed its source and a website that you can visit if you would like to conduct your own research. Please remember to critically evaluate any sources that you consult and consider whether the information you are viewing is accurate and unbiased.

The Modern Families Index 2017

An extract from **The Modern Families Index.**

The *Modern Families Index* is a snapshot of how working families in the UK manage the balance between family life and work. The *Index* asks them what their family and work balance is like, whether or not the balance they have matches their aspirations, and what the effects of being a working parent and an employee are on family life. How much time do families spend together, and what is the quality of that time? Are parents able to leave work at work, or do they bring it home with them? In couple families, how do parents share working and caring and is this changing between the generations? And do parents feel that their employer and government are doing enough to help them combine work and family? The *Index* is not a study of a particular group of parents, but seeks to capture the experiences of 'everyday' families, however configured. It describes the pressure points where family and work meet today, and how these vary by demographic and other circumstances. Learning from what parents who have completed the *Index* say, based on the reality of their experience, shows us what is working for working families, and what needs to change – to inform the policy landscape, configuration of the labour market and employment practice in the UK.

Families in the UK today

In 2016, there were 4.8 million married (opposite and same sex) or civil partner couple families with dependent children in the UK. There were 1.3 million cohabiting couples with dependent children and 1.9 million single parent families with dependent children. Women accounted for 86 per cent of single parents with dependent children and men the remaining 14 per cent

Of the 13.9 million dependent children living in families, the majority (63 per cent) of dependent children live in a married couple family. The percentage of dependent children living in cohabiting families increased from seven per cent to 15 per cent between 1996 and 2016, while the percentage of dependent children living in single parent families changed little. Married couples with dependent children have more children on average than other family types. In 2016, 55 per cent of single parents with dependent children had one child, whereas 39 per cent of married couples with dependent children had one child.

Working patterns

Dual-earner households are now the norm in the UK: in 2014 in more than 68 per cent of couple families both parents were working. Among couple families, the percentage of both parents working full time increased from 26 per cent in 2001 to 31 per cent in 2013.

In 2014, 96 per cent of couple families with one or two dependent children had one or both parents working. This reduces slightly to 91 per cent of couple families with three or more dependent children.

Similarly, in 2014, 65 per cent of single parents with one or two dependent children were working compared with 47 per cent of single parents with three or more dependent children. Couple parents with young children (aged under five) were almost twice (78.6 per cent) as likely to be in employment as single parents with young children (40.9 per cent).

The Institute for Public Policy Research reported that, since the extension of the right to request flexible working in 2014, 36 per cent of women in employment with children under six have requested more flexible hours, with 80 per cent of requests either partially or fully agreed.

Qualitative studies show that fathers in employment feel marginalised from access to flexible working opportunities, due to their managers' assumption that they are the breadwinners. Studies also show that mothers working flexibly, including part time, tend to be side-lined or downgraded. For both mothers and fathers there is a gap between policy and practice with regard to flexible working.

Turning to types of occupation, in 2014 single mothers with dependent children were more likely to work in low-skilled jobs such as cleaning and catering than mothers living in couple households. More than 14 per cent of single mothers were employed in low-skilled occupations, compared with eight per cent of mothers in a couple relationship. 40 per cent of mothers in a couple relationship worked in higher skilled occupations like nursing or teaching, compared with 17 per cent of single mothers.

There has been a change in fathers' working hours in the UK. Although they still work some of the longest hours in Europe, their hours have fallen from 47 hours per week in 2001 to 45 hours per week in 2011. There has also been a significant change in the proportion of fathers working 48 hours or more. In 2001, 40 per cent of fathers in the UK worked 48 hours or more. However, this proportion declined to 31 per cent by 2013.

While mothers tend to perform more routine family activities and be more involved with children than fathers, it is clear that fathers' involvement with children has grown and is growing. Their involvement in childcare increased from less than 15 minutes a day in the mid-1970s to three hours a day during the week by the late 1990s. In 2005, fathers did a third of parental childcare within households.

Income

The average UK salary for a full-time employee in April 2016 was £28,200.

According to the Joseph Rowntree Foundation in 2016, a single parent with one child (pre-school and primary age) needed to earn at least £27,909 a year before tax to achieve the minimum income standard (how much income households need to afford an acceptable standard of living). Couples with two children (pre-school and primary age) need to earn at least £18,906 each before tax.

It is estimated to cost £152,000 in two parent families and £183,000 in single parent families to bring up a child. By 2014/15 the number of children in poverty had increased by 60,000 from 2002/03 to 3.9 million. Children in single parent families are more likely to live in poverty (44 per cent of children) than in couple parent families (24 per cent).

Childcare

The use of formal childcare in the UK is high. 68 per cent of families use childcare, with 42 per cent of families using more than one type of childcare. Informal care plays a significant role in childcare – grandparental care is most commonly used (31 per cent).

The cost of nursery part time (25 hours) is £117 per week, or £6,100 per year, a one per cent rise since 2015. A registered childminder now costs £104.27 per week for part-time care for a child under two, compared with £104.06 in 2015. Childcare costs account for a significant proportion of family expenditure. For example, a family with one child under two in part-time childcare and one child at an after-school club can now expect to pay £7,900 per year for childcare, which is over 28 per cent of median household income in the UK.

Women still take a disproportionate amount of responsibility for unpaid care work within households.

Analysis of time-use data shows that women carry out an average of 60 per cent more unpaid work than men. On average, men spend 16 hours a week doing unpaid care work including childcare, laundry and cleaning, compared to women (26 hours a week). The gendered division of labour within households is a barrier to women's participation in the labour market. While only one per cent of men aged

16 to 64 were economically inactive due to unpaid care work, ten per cent of women aged 16 to 64 stayed out of work to look after the family or home. The high cost of childcare has a great influence on parents' choices, particularly mothers, to give up work or reduce their working hours.

Key findings

⇨ Only one in five families said they have got the right balance between time (to spend with family) and money (earning or having enough income) to see their family thrive. More than a third say they haven't got enough time or money.

⇨ In couple families, many parents both work full time. 48 per cent of couple families in the survey said they both worked full time. 57 per cent of single parents worked full time.

⇨ Just under half of parents (47 per cent) think that over the last two years it has become financially more difficult to raise a family.

⇨ Family life is under pressure from work. The majority of parents (72 per cent) catch up on work at home in the evenings and at weekends, with 41 per cent saying this is often or all the time.

⇨ Only a third of parents manage to leave work on time every day. For many, staying later at work is a regular occurrence. One in five parents working full time is putting in five extra weeks a year – the equivalent of their annual holiday allowance – in unpaid work, just to keep up with the demands of the job. A third of working parents regularly feel burnt out.

⇨ Almost half (48 per cent) said working hours regularly got in the way of spending time with their children. A third said that work pressure negatively affected their relationship with their partner and a quarter said it led to rows with their children.

⇨ Parents are keen to mitigate the effects of work on family life. They identified flexible working as a key way of getting a better balance, but many felt that they could not make use of it because of their job, manager's attitude or workplace culture.

⇨ Parents are worried about discussing family and work-related issues with their employers. 41 per cent said they had lied or bent the truth to their employer about family life conflicting with work, and almost half said they were not comfortable talking about work boundaries with their employer.

⇨ Fathers increasingly see themselves as actively involved in childcare, and will make career sacrifices accordingly: 69 per cent of fathers said they would consider their childcare arrangements before they took a new job or promotion. Fathers are the more likely (47 per cent) to want to downshift into a less stressful job and 38 per cent would be willing to take a pay cut to achieve a better work-life balance, reflecting the difficulty they face in reconciling work and home life.

⇨ Parents said they would leave employers who do not offer good work-life balance opportunities. Improved opportunities for better work-life balance and a better work-life balance culture were priorities. In contrast, parents said that employers who afforded them a good work-life balance would get more motivated, loyal and productive employees.

⇨ The above extract is reprinted with kind permission from Working Families. Please visit www.workingfamilies.org.uk for further information.

© 2018 Working Families

More mothers with young children working full-time

Mothers with young children are more likely to go back to or begin full-time work now than 20 years ago, new ONS analysis suggests.

The proportion of mothers with children aged between three and four who are in employment increased by almost ten percentage points over the past two decades. In England there are now around 133,000 more mothers, whose youngest child is a toddler, in employment in 2017 (65.1%), compared with 1997 (55.8%). This was largely driven by an increase in full-time employment.

This analysis comes as the Government expanded the provision of free childcare from 15 to 30 hours a week in England. The policy is designed to help boost employment for parents, particularly mothers, looking to return to work or increase their working hours.

More mothers with young children working full-time

The rise in overall employment for mothers has been driven mainly by an increasing number working in full-time employment. The proportion of mothers working part-time when they have young children has remained relatively static over the period, although it remains much higher than those working full-time.

However, mothers with young children have the lowest employment levels of all parents with dependent children at 65.1%. In comparison, the employment rate of fathers with children aged three or four is 93.2%.

More fathers with young children working part-time

The introduction of flexible working practices and shared parental leave have also made it easier for fathers to share childcare responsibilities. ONS data reflects this social change to an extent. There is a marked increase in the number of fathers who have young children working part-time – it has almost doubled from 3.9% in 1997 to 6.9% in 2017.

However, this is still well below the proportion of women with young children working part-time – 38.2% in 2017. Generally, the rate of men with young children working full-time has remained stable, and their overall employment is less affected by parenthood compared with women.

Policy changes may have affected parental employment

The doubling of free childcare from 15 hours a week to 30 hours in England is just one of a larger number of initiatives designed to improve education, make childcare more affordable, and to encourage parents back into work.

26 September 2017

⇨ The above is reprinted with kind permission from the Office for National Statistics. Please visit www.visual.ons.gov.uk for further information.

© Crown copyright 2018

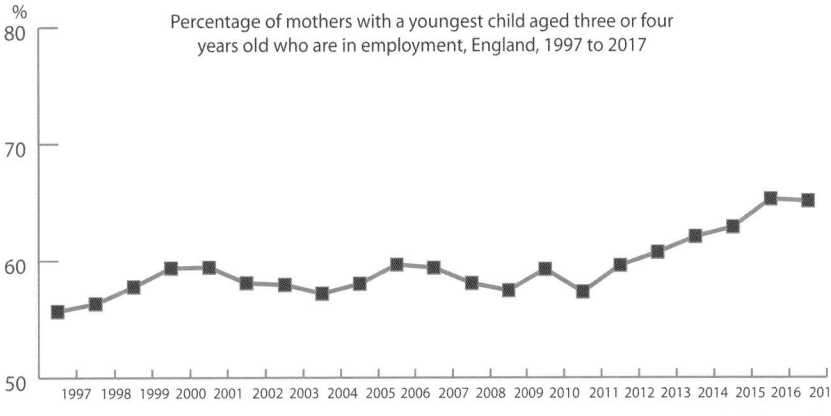

Percentage of mothers with a youngest child aged three or four years old who are in employment, England, 1997 to 2017

Source: Labour Force Survey Household datasets, ONS

Being a working mother is not bad for your children

An article from **The Conversation.**

THE CONVERSATION

By Markus Klein, Lecturer on Human Development and Education Policy, Strathclyde University and Michael Kühhirt, Lecturer in Sociology, University of Cologne

The question of whether mothers should work or stay at home in their children's early years has always been a hot potato in the media, provoking strong emotions and headlines including: "Sorry working mums, daycare is bad for your kid" or "The case for working mothers: your kids will be just fine."

The possible benefits and risks of mothers' working on children's well-being is highly politicised and is the perennial subject of heated scientific and public debate. As policies designed to bring mothers into the workforce are on the increase – and pressure on women from all sides continues to mount – it is important to know how the children of working mothers are actually faring.

Whether mothers decide to stay at home or go back to work after they've given birth, how old their child is when they decide to return to work and how many hours they are working are all important factors in the developmental environment.

By bringing in money and raising the overall family income, working mothers may be able to provide a more stimulating and safer environment for their children. This isn't just a matter of more expensive toys or learning material but also better living conditions, better nutrition and reduced family stress.

However, long working hours and work-related stress could have an impact on the quality and quantity of interactions mothers can have with their children – interactions that are crucial for developing cognitive skills and language growth.

A dynamic perspective

In our recent study – published in the journal *Child Development* – we looked at 2,200 children of the Growing Up in Scotland study, who were born in 2005/2006 and were followed from roughly ten months old until around their fifth birthday. The mothers' employment history and other family characteristics were collected through yearly surveys throughout the first five years of the child's life.

As a measure of their vocabulary at the age of five, children were asked to name objects from a picture booklet. Reasoning ability at age five was established by asking children to find similarities between a given image and objects displayed in a picture book.

Unlike most previous research which measured women's employment at a particular time, for example when their child was a year old, our study captured maternal employment throughout their child's first five years and the effect this had on the child's development.

We found that a mother's employment history doesn't have a positive or negative impact (see page 22) on a child's reasoning ability or vocabulary at five years old. The reason for this is that children's cognitive and language skills are shaped by individual traits and environmental conditions that can change many times throughout childhood. Therefore, development and well-being at a certain age are the result of children's cumulative experiences over their first few years, not simply a result of a single snapshot moment.

Given that circumstances can change many times over – with mothers going in and out of employment or changes in pay, working hours and conditions – the constantly evolving nature of child development is important to consider when it comes to measuring any effect.

Any impact of a mother's employment on children's cognitive skills and language growth, via family income or parent-child interactions, is likely to unfold only if mothers continue to be employed for a longer period of time. Long-term stability in any status may also help families to develop strategies that work for their specific child, whereas frequent changes may be harmful in establishing a routine that works.

Our study advances the existing research by measuring both the complexity of mothers' work history and their typical employment patterns – distinguishing between full-time employed, part-time employed, or not working, in each year.

Women making it work

We did find small differences in cognitive ability and vocabulary growth between children whose mothers followed different employment patterns. But for the most part, these differences seem to be driven by other characteristics, such as mothers' education or the number of siblings, which influence a mother's decision to work in the first five years after birth.

In other words, children with similar family characteristics develop comparable cognitive and vocabulary abilities even if their mothers' work histories differ vastly in the first five years after birth.

Both the exaggerated claims of benefits and the harmful effects of working mothers on their children are not supported by our research, at least when it comes to early language acquisition and reasoning ability. We found that mothers manage to combine their careers with careful consideration of their children's development – and that being in employment itself is not a major driver of differences in children's outcomes.

From a policy perspective, these results support the role of initiatives that aim to raise the rates of mothers in work, such as the plan to increase provision of free early learning and childcare to 1,140 hours by 2020 in Scotland.

All policies that enable women to choose whether they go back into work or not should be encouraged. However, it's the ability to make choices that work for the individual that matter – pressure on women one way or the other is not going to improve the development of their children.

28 July 2017

⇨ The above is reprinted with kind permission from *The Conversation*. Please visit www.theconversation. com for further information.

© 2010-2018 The Conversation Trust (UK)

UK parents no longer work the longest hours in EU

Fathers in the UK are no longer working the longest hours in Europe, according to a study of 17 countries published by NatCen Social Research, Thomas Coram Research Unit (TCRU, UCL Institute of Education) and the University of East Anglia (UEA).

Workers in the UK once had the longest week in the EU, but a decline since 2001 in average working hours among fathers means this is no longer the case. In 2001, fathers in the UK worked an average of 46.1 hours per week. By 2013, this had decreased to 43 hours (including part-time workers).

Meanwhile, the average working week for all British mothers, including those who work part-time, has increased from 26.8 to 29.1 hours in the same time period.

In 2013, the highest average weekly full-time working hours were found in Greece for both fathers (46 hours) and mothers (over 41 hours). UK fathers working full-time had the second longest hours on average (44.6), whereas full-time mothers worked on average 39.5 hours per week.

Three in ten UK fathers regularly work over 48 hours per week, down from four in ten in 2001. Greece now leads the EU in long working hours, with 40% of fathers working over 48 hours per week.

Changing patterns of work

The research also found significant shifts in the working patterns of parents across Europe since the recession:

⇨ The proportion of UK households where both parents work full

time increased from 26.4% in 2001 to 30.8% in 2013.

⇨ The proportion of UK households where neither parent works decreased from 6% in 2001 to 4.8% in 2013.

⇨ In the UK there has been a significant decline in the proportion of fathers doing shift work or working evenings or nights. The proportion of fathers who usually work at weekends has increased significantly, while mothers' weekend and shift work has remained the same.

⇨ In 16 of the 17 countries studied, the proportion of sole male breadwinner households decreased – only in Slovakia did the proportion increase.

⇨ In countries that were most affected by the recession, the proportion of workless households significantly increased. In Greece, for example, the proportion of workless households increased from 2.4% in 2001 to 9.9% in 2013.

Professor Margaret O'Brien, Director of the Thomas Coram Research Unit, UCL Institute of Education said: "This research highlights the variety in family working practices across Europe and how this has changed over the last decade, a period that includes the Great Recession."

Dr Svetlana Speight, Research Director at NatCen Social Research said: "This new data builds on what we already knew about modern fatherhood: that the sole male breadwinner model is in decline across Europe. Mothers are now more likely to work and, in the UK, more likely to work full-time, at the same time as fathers are working a shorter week, which allows them to take on more childcare responsibilities."

Dr Matthew Aldrich, Lecturer in Economics and Associate Dean for Employability for the Social Science Faculty, UEA said: "Whilst some countries were shielded from the effects of the recession, families in most European countries used a myriad of responses to the challenging labour market – particularly the use of non-standard working patterns and working hours."

7 April 2016

⇨ The above is reprinted with kind permission from Institute of Education. This work was supported by the Economic and Social Reasearch Council [grant number ES/KOO3739/1]. Please visit www. http://www. modernfatherhood.org/wp-content/uploads/2016/03/Parental-Working-in-Europe-Working-Hours-final_formatv3.pdf for further information.

© 2018 Institute of Education

My work-life balance problems

For 20 years, Louise Chunn worked full-time and was a part-time mother of three. Would she recommend the same balance to her daughters?

Louise Chunn

I have always been a proselytiser for working mothers. How could I not be? For four years in the 90s, I edited *The Guardian's* women's pages and launched the parents pages in *G2*. My mother ran several of her own businesses, and her mother, too, for a while. Work to me denoted independence, adventure, glamour and, of course, money. As long as I could afford to employ reliable childcare, why would I want to walk away from all of that?

It is only recently that I have been able to acknowledge that mixing work and children comes with its downsides. Why did it take me so long? Part of me doggedly believed I had to stick to my line. But I have to admit that another part didn't want to examine what the effect of more than 20 years of working motherhood has had on my children.

My first child, Charlie, was born in March 1986 and I started back full-time on the newly launched fashion magazine *Elle* when he was six months old. Two and a quarter years later, I gave birth to Alice and bounced back to work even sooner, as I feared my job might not be open if I took longer maternity leave (no one who wanted to be taken seriously took the full amount in those days). Before my two had even started school I had separated from their father, so my career in journalism became less about creative fulfilment and more about paying my way. I felt I couldn't not work, but then I very much wanted to work, so I never really considered any other options.

For the next ten years, I powered through jobs at *The Guardian*, *Vogue* and the *London Evening Standard*. To pick up my children from school and look after them during the holidays, I employed a series of nannies from Australia, Hungary, Scotland, New Zealand, the Czech Republic, Slovenia, Brazil, wherever. Mostly they didn't live with us – the children and I preferred it

that way – and mostly we all got along pretty well. We even had a 'manny' for a while.

But then my long-term boyfriend and I bought a house together, had a daughter, Isabel, and married. We had just stopped employing nannies – both the older children were at secondary school – when it started all over again. Issy was five months old when I got a job at *InStyle* magazine as deputy editor. In the following years I edited that magazine and then Good Housekeeping – both full-time, full-on jobs. Since November, however, I have been a freelance journalist and editorial consultant. And the painful truth about my new life is that my children love it.

It's obvious perhaps, but what I give them now, which I rarely could before, is my attention. Yes, I would spend time with Issy while she practised piano in the morning but one eye was always on the clock – and my brain was already in combat mode for the office. How else to explain the many times I arrived at work with her lunchbox or PE kit still stuffed in my bag because I wasn't concentrating on her day, but mine?

And just because the other two are older doesn't mean I couldn't do much better. Alice might have been able to speak to me from her college room 50 miles away, but I would generally be in a taxi, reading a page proof or a BlackBerry message at the same time. When she was at home during university holidays, I couldn't once join her for an excavation of Top Shop's finest merchandise. Too busy, busy, busy.

You'll note I am not talking about missing my children's first words or their first steps. I am not terribly sentimental or guilt-ridden about their babyhood. In fact, in inverse proportion to many women I know, I feel that the

older children get, the more important it is to keep an eye on their progress. A friend's wise mother agrees. Asked whether babies or teenagers were the hardest, this 70-something matriarch replied: "I found the years between 20 and 25 the worst." I can see why. You're looking at the rest of their lives. There is everything to play for and you have to manoeuvre your children much more subtly as they get older, planting ideas rather than making demands or rules.

My son did not, I believe, have a happy time at university. He was living away from home for the first time and did not easily overcome the isolation. You could say (and I did) that there wasn't much I could do about it. Universities do not suffer mothers ringing up with vague concerns about fitting in. I would phone him and he would barely respond to my questions. It worried me greatly, yet after five minutes or so I would simply hang up and get back to work. Given the time again, it would be different. Never mind the four-hour drive, I would visit him. And visit again and again, until I felt he was on the road to coping. The fact that he is now gainfully employed and happily living away from home makes me feel better, but not entirely off the hook.

This week, Alice and I sat in our kitchen having lunch. She has just graduated from Oxford and is looking for work to finance some travel in the future. We spend a lot of time talking about work at the moment, so I queried her feelings about my past work/life balance. "I've always felt proud of your jobs. Because you weren't pushing me all the time like some of my friends' mothers did, I think I ended up motivating myself more."

And the minuses? There was quite a long pause, as befits a sensitive issue. "I suppose I think you could have been more involved in my life along the way. I didn't get much time with you – and certainly not once Issy was born." Since I stopped full-time work, we've had several holidays together, including one bonding spa break that she loved.

For Issy, the change in circumstances has been the most dramatic. I don't think I even had a mobile phone until the older two were at secondary school but Issy's life coincided with my time as a glossy magazine editor. At *InStyle*, I was away for two to three weeks every six months, staying in glamorous hotels, watching fashion shows, drinking a bottle of wine or two with magazine friends at the end of a hard, long day – not seeing her for days and nights on end. At *Good Housekeeping* I would rarely be home before 7pm, usually still tapping something into my BlackBerry as I walked in the door.

I kept her nanny on for a long time after I finished there. She and Simona were very close and I didn't want to disrupt her routine. But a few weeks ago we parted company and Issy and I set off into the summer without a nanny safety net. I've always dropped her at school in the morning but on the first day of the new regime I asked rather nervously, "What time does your class get out?" She sighed, looked around at her pals' frankly shocked faces, and quipped: "Three-thirty, Mum – and I don't like brussels sprouts!"

Regrets, I have a few – but the truth is, for most of my full-time working mother life I did not have the 'luxury' of chucking in the towel when family problems impinged. I was a single mother with no immediate family in this country and I was expected to (and felt it right that I should) fend for myself. In the 80s and 90s there was very little opportunity for part-time or flexible working in the media if you were remotely ambitious. And the pay was paltry. But I did on one occasion switch jobs when Alice, then six, told me that she wanted me to pick her up from school, even just one day a week. For the same salary, I went from a high-pressure daily newspaper where I had responsibility for a section to a four-day week on a magazine where I was part of a large team. For a year it worked beautifully, but when a promotion was offered it came with

a fifth day attached. I barely hesitated before accepting. Alice was initially annoyed that I was no longer going to be the one to collect her from school on that precious one day a week. But when I mentioned that the change brought a company car that would start every time rather than limping on with AA breakdown cover she understood.

Looking back, I think the big question for many women of my age was: will having children affect my chances of having a career? At *Elle* I was one of only two women with children, and we barely ever talked about them. There were certainly no cereal-smeared grinning baby photos on our desks. We felt we had to tread carefully, not making demands or drawing attention to the complications in our lives, lest the feminist battle be lost and we be pitched back into a life of domestic drudgery we imagined might lie in wait.

Now it has switched to: how will my job affect my child? The timetable of the nursery or childminder can seem paramount; the maternity leave can be extended to a year; most requests for flexible working are now granted. And mothers fret – loudly and openly – about leaving their children and how guilty it makes them feel.

In December 2008, a wide-ranging Cabinet Office study revealed that about 25% of adults aged 30 to 59 have downsized their careers over the last ten years by quitting their jobs, reducing their hours or changing their career path, a third of them saying that spending more time with their family was the primary reason.

Shortly after that, Julia Hobsbawm's book, *The See-Saw 100 Ideas for Work-Life Balance*, was the trigger for a standing room-only editorial intelligence discussion on the topic at the Cass Business School.

While Hobsbawm (a mother of three) looks to employers and the Government to come up with ways to make the plight of working parents easier, Dr Nicola Brewer, departing chief executive of the Equality and Human Rights Commission, pointed out that it was an "inconvenient truth" that extended maternity leave was

threatening women's progress in the workplace. In former jobs, I was responsible for the hiring of large numbers of women who were either mothers already or else possibly thinking of joining that blessed group in the near future. So I know what she is talking about. It isn't easy to get work done when significant numbers are on maternity leave or working flexible hours – and it isn't always fair on their child-free colleagues either. I still fear that pushing too hard on maternity leave will erode women's desirability in the workplace. In fact, when Alice and I talk about her future career, I counsel her to find an area where having a family is not seen as a disadvantage.

Meanwhile, at my house, life is radically different. The newly acquired biscuit tins are being filled – Nigel Slater's chocolate brownies are my latest triumph – there's always clean underwear and I open the post when it actually arrives. My husband is happy to no longer get "I'm sorry, I'm still in the office" calls after I'm due home, I'm in regular contact with my family in New Zealand and friends are seen, talked to, laughed with. I do work, but not so all-consumingly. I have time to prune, feed and smell the roses, and I have time to watch my children grow.

That doesn't mean I don't ever want to work like a fiend again – really committing to producing something as part of a team is a joy and a thrill. But maybe my 20-plus years of working motherhood is not such a great thing to crow about after all. I wouldn't deny any other woman the chance to step into my working-day stilettos, but I would softly whisper, "Are you sure that it's the right thing to do, for everyone, and not just you?"

21 October 2017

⇨ The above is reprinted with kind permission from *The Guardian*. Please visit www.theguardian.com for further information.

© 2018 Guardian News and Media Limited

Why it's not true to say just 1% of dads have taken up shared parental leave

The statistic includes men who weren't eligible for SPL.

By Amy Packham

On the first anniversary of the launch of Shared Parental Leave (SPL), it has been widely reported that just 1% of dads have chosen to take it up.

However this figure, taken from research compiled by My Family Care, which helps businesses introduce family friendly ways of working, and the Women's Business Council, has been misreported.

There were 200 employers interviewed for the research and from these companies, just 1% of male employees took up SPL.

My Family Care has pointed out that the figure included men who didn't have children or adopt in the last year, so would not have been eligible to take up SPL.

"It's important to note that we have reported the figures against ALL male employees as the majority of companies were unable to tell us the size of their male populations that were eligible for Shared Parental Leave," the company stated.

A spokesperson for the Department of Business, Innovation and Skills said the Government will be evaluating the policy in 2018 to enable them to accurately estimate the take up of Shared Parental Leave.

"When the policy was introduced, the Government estimated that around 285,000 couples would be eligible for SPL and that the take up would be between 2% and 8%," the spokesperson told The Huffington Post UK.

"Take up is likely to be higher in organisations that offer pay above the statutory minimum."

The policy, which allows couples to share leave following the birth of a baby or adoption of a child, was introduced in 2015.

The aim of the policy was to help new mums get back into the workplace and give men the opportunity to care full time for their new baby or adopted child in the first year.

Alongside surveying companies, My Family Care and the Women's Business Council also surveyed 1,000 men and women who were parents or parents-to-be about their views on SPL.

These findings gave some insight into people's attitudes towards SPL, one year after it was launched.

Many women said they would be reluctant to share their leave, with an estimated 55% admitting they didn't want to cut their time with a new baby short.

Just over half of respondents (50% of men and 57% of women) said they believed that taking SPL could negatively impact on a man's career.

From those surveyed, 80% of both men and women agreed that a decision to share leave would be dependent on their finances and their employer's enhancement of SPL.

However, My Family Care did find that men are interested in taking SPL in the future, with almost two thirds (63%) who are considering having more children saying it was likely they would choose to take SPL.

Ben Black, founder of My Family Care told The Huffington Post UK, he's optimistic about the policy's uptake in the future.

"This is all new – give it a bit of time," he said.

"Businesses need to lose the fear. Shared Parental Leave will involve men taking a month off here and there.

"The world won't collapse and careers will remain on track.

"And also society needs to grow up; this is the most difficult one to get past.

"Men need to stop worrying about how they are perceived and women need to let go."

Of the 200 employers asked, 48% were "optimistic" about SPL, believing it will be normalised over time, while 45% thought it would remain a minority choice.

Black believes dads are more likely to take up SPL if their employers are more understanding.

"Businesses need to help their employees combine work and family, by providing them with choices and enabling them to carry on with their careers while having a family," he added.

"More and more we're going to hear fantastic stories of fathers who have taken SPL.

"Once these stories filter through, and the notion of sharing leave in this way becomes 'normal', then it will be accepted practice.

"Of course, all change takes time and while it hasn't so far been the cultural change that many were clamouring for, I suspect with many companies enhancing paternity leave, momentum will grow."

Emer Timmons, chair of the 'Men as Change Agents' working group at the Women's Business Council said the findings highlight the important role businesses can play in raising awareness of the opportunity to take SPL.

"We can see that some fathers have embraced the opportunity to spend time with their young families but that there is still a long way to go for others," he said.

"Increasing flexibility in the workplace is a key recommendation of the Women's Business Council – it is good for women, good for families, good for business and ultimately the economy, so it's a win-win situation all round."

Tom Picton-Turbervill, senior manager in Tax at Deloitte was one of the fathers who did take up SPL after his son Henry was born in June 2015.

His main aim for taking leave was to support his wife and build up a relationship with his son, Henry, who is now nine months old.

He took the initial two weeks paternity leave when his son was born and then four weeks SPL, together with his wife, during August 2015.

"Babies change so quickly in those first few months and I wanted to be there to experience it," he explained.

"Taking the time out has given me confidence in looking after my son. My wife and I learned how to be parents together rather than me trying to catch up at weekends and evenings.

"The time off allowed me to spend time with him and my wife in those first few weeks, watching him develop.

"My colleagues at work were really supportive of me taking the time off and a common reaction was 'I wish this was around when I had my kids'."

5 April 2016

⇨ The above is reprinted with kind permission from *The Huffington Post*. Please visit www.huffingtonpost.co.uk for further information.

© 2018 AOL (UK) Limited

Children object to losing time with fathers to 24/7 economy

Weekdays are OK, but children resent their fathers working nights, weekends and in stressful, inflexible jobs.

By Professor Lyndall Strazdins

Fathers struggle to strike a work-family balance. According to some studies, many find it tougher than even mothers do. Women also complain about dads overworking – particularly when they're left holding the baby or if family commitments mean they can't compete at work with "long-hours men". But how do children feel about dads' jobs?

We asked thousands of children between ten and 13-years-old. Their responses are a wake-up call to governments who often regard fathers' work simply in relation to family income but rarely in relation to family time. Unlike mothers, fathers have received little effective consideration from workplaces or policy makers to help them achieve family-friendly work.

That oversight is a big problem for children, our study finds. It shows that work often encroaches unacceptably on children's relationships with their dads. Indeed childhood is at odds with many aspects of the evolving 24/7 economy.

Children accept that dads need to work

It's not that children are unrealistic and think dad should be around for them all the time. They accept him going to work. But they don't like the job getting in the way of special times with him – weekends and evenings. They object when work so stresses him out that he's not much fun as a parent or when it's so inflexible that he can't be there for them at important times.

"Children don't want their dads to work weekends, evenings or nights, they also feel stress when their dad's work is high pressure, and they object when their fathers don't have flexibility around work times"

We found that few of the thousands of children we surveyed wished that their father didn't work at all. Most valued fathers' employment. They accepted that it restricted their dads' time. They considered jobs to be important and a benefit to their family. But there came a tipping point when the demands of their fathers' working life made them protective of their time with him. Children don't want their dads to work weekends, evenings or nights. They also feel stress when their dad's work is high pressured, and they object when their fathers don't have flexibility around work times.

These constraints on time with dad – about which children expressed discontent – also corresponded with declines in children's estimation of how close they felt to their fathers. That's a concern because a large body of evidence shows that close relationships between fathers and their children are fundamental to children's well-being – their identity, developmental achievement and long-term health.

"Policy makers should seek solutions in the operation of the labour market, rather than leaving fathers to push back against workplace expectations, and, if they do, take the risk that they will pay a high price"

Overall, the findings reinforce evidence from elsewhere that children view time with their fathers as central, special and unique, especially time together at weekends, whereas long weekday hours are viewed as part of the job, up to a point.

Study design

Our study paired the work practices and hours of more than 2,500 Australian fathers with the views of their children, aged 10 to 13. The fathers were all part of intact families. Separated dads and their children, who may face an even more varied set of work-family dilemmas, were not included in the study.

We found that problematic workplace demands were not confined to fathers in high pressure, long-hours, high-earning jobs. Our study particularly highlighted concerns among the children of low-income fathers. They objected when their fathers' work was scheduled on evenings, night and weekends and where start or stop times were inflexible. Children of such fathers are caught between a rock and a hard place. As a 16-year-old said in another study, "I really can't pick because we need the money, but I also need my parents."

Boys tended to object more than girls do to work demands on their fathers. One possible explanation is that boys may look at their fathers' working lives and see a future that they don't wish for themselves.

Many fathers have difficulty securing flexible daytime jobs that produce sufficient income for their families. Yet family research into labour markets tends to focus on how workplace practices disadvantage women in terms of pay and employment. Little research has tested how the requirements of fathers' jobs affect children's experiences. By looking at fathers, we have shown that the same work-time processes that underpin gender inequality also cause problems for children.

Work practices that trouble children are widespread

We also found that fathers' concerns about particular work practices or schedules are broadly similar to their children's. Yet the work practices that cause problems for both were widespread in the families we studied. Nearly half of the fathers worked more than 45 hours a week, one quarter regularly worked weekends, and a fifth worked evenings, nights, or irregular or rotating schedules. Two in five worked in jobs considered to be high pressured, and more than a third lacked flexibility

around when they started or stopped. Half of the fathers missed family events because of work, and about a fifth described their family time as more pressured and less fun because of their jobs.

Work practices are making life unhappy for many dads and their children. But we rarely hear about the issue, and policy does little to alleviate it. The problem tends to be left to individual fathers to resolve. Yet many of them have no real choice. Instead, they struggle with the dilemma of how to earn enough for their families, stay competitive in the job market and care for their children in the way that they – and the kids – would like.

The widespread nature of the problem – and the shared concerns of fathers, children and (we know from other studies) mothers – suggests that policy makers should seek solutions in the operation of the labour market, rather than leaving fathers to push back against workplace expectations, and, if they do, take the risk that they will pay a high price.

3 July 2017

⇨ The above is reprinted with kind permission from Child and Family Blog. Please visit www.childandfamilyblog.com for further information.

© 2018 Child and Family Blog

Paternity leave: how Britain compares with the rest of the world

Does the UK policy on paternity leave stand up to the rest of the world?

By Guy Kelly

A new incentive was launched in Sweden this week encouraging fathers to take three months paid paternity leave. Like several European countries, Sweden has a 'daddy quota' of paid time off that's allocated to couples as a unit, but only allowed to be taken by the father and therefore lost if he chooses not to take it. The new 30-day extension, which came into force on 1 January, follows a successful increase to two months in 2002.

It's a policy designed to ensure men take more of the childcare burden, and the latest change is expected to be embraced by fathers in Sweden, which was the first to introduce gender-indifferent parental leave in 1974. Already, men there take an average of three months off work to look after their newborns; in Britain less than 10% exceed the statutory two weeks, often citing a fear of falling behind in the rat race.

Currently UK fathers are eligible to take one or two weeks paid leave any time within 56 days of the birth. As a result of changes championed by Nick Clegg in 2014, there is also an option of taking between two and 26 additional weeks off, with each extra week subtracted from your partner's remaining allocation.

The Scandinavian stances on parental leave – as with so many other social policies – may make the UK's seem staid and imbalanced, then, but how do our rights compare with fathers around the world?

Spain

The Spanish are typically relaxed with their parental policies: men are allowed 15 days paid, while new parents are then permitted a whopping three years unpaid. The catch, however, is that employers can change their absentee's role after a year off.

United States

There is no federal paid parental leave (or maternity) in the US, making it one of the few developed countries in the world lacking state support for new parents, though many states have their own systems.

Corporate policies can be very generous, too: last year Facebook brought male employees' paid leave in line with women's, meaning any new parent working at the social media company around the world is permitted four months of leave. Meanwhile Netflix allows unlimited paid time off for one year.

France

We beat the French, at least: new fathers across the channel are permitted 11 days paid leave, with an additional six months available without pay.

Iceland

Icelandic fathers receive 90 days off after their baby's birth, at a rate of around 80% of their salary, with a further three months to share with their partners.

South Korea

To address the shame of being placed 115th of 145 in the World Economic Forum's gender equality index, paternity leave has become a key issue in South Korea, where the Government intends to increase the ratio of men taking leave to 30% over the next 15 years. Mothers and fathers there are entitled to the same amount of time off (a year) partially paid.

Japan

A year's unpaid leave is on offer to both parents, but hardly any dads take it: as of 2014, only 1.9% availed themselves of the time off.

Germany

One of the more generous policies in Europe, German men and women have equal rights to parental leave of 12 to 14 months on 65% of the individual parent's salary.

Norway

Like Sweden, Norway employs a 'use it or lose it' system, with 14 weeks (two more than new Swedish policy, even) available to new parents, but they lose the allocation collectively if fathers don't accept their share of the burden.

6 January 2016

⇨ The above extract is reprinted with kind permission from *The Telegraph*. Please visit www. telegraph.co.uk for further information.

© Telegraph Media Group Limited 2014

One in three families are a month's pay from losing homes, says study

Shelter finds that 37% of working families in England could not cover housing costs for more than a month in event of job loss.

By Patrick Collinson, Money Editor

More than one in three families in England are a monthly pay packet away from losing their homes, according to research by Shelter highlighting how many households have almost no savings.

The housing charity found that 37% of working families would be unable to cover their housing costs for more than a month if one partner lost their job.

The findings mirror government figures, which show that there are 16.5 million working-age adults in the UK with no savings.

Campbell Robb, the chief executive of Shelter, said: "These figures are a stark reminder that sky-high housing costs are leaving millions of working families stretched to breaking point and barely scraping by from one pay cheque to the next.

"Any one of us could hit a bump along life's road, and at Shelter, we speak to parents every day who, after losing their job or seeing their hours cut, are terrified of losing the roof over their children's heads too."

The charity is calling for an improved welfare safety net to prevent families where someone loses a job from "hurtling towards homelessness".

The phenomenon of the working poor, those earning a regular salary, but living from one pay cheque to the next with no savings to speak of, is a widespread feature in English-speaking western economies such as the UK, Canada, the US and Australia.

An annual survey by US website Bankrate found that 63% of Americans have no emergency savings for necessities such as a $1,000 (£770) emergency room visit or a $500 car repair. Most turn to credit cards when financial disaster looms.

According to the US Federal Reserve board, 47% of Americans would have trouble finding $400 for an emergency expense.

Writing in *The Atlantic* about the "secret shame" of middle-class Americans, the author Neal Gabler said he shared their difficulties, juggling creditors to make it through the week.

"I know what it is like to dread going to the mailbox, because there will always be new bills to pay, but seldom a cheque with which to pay them," he wrote.

Martin Lewis of MoneySavingExpert. com says in his book *The Money Diet*: "In truth we should all have three to six months' income saved away, so that we're ready for any emergency."

But he acknowledges that this is easier said than done. Many savings accounts pay virtually zero interest after the Bank of England cut the base rate to 0.25% last week.

Losing a job and relationship breakdown are among the chief reasons for households falling into serious debt.

Shelter cites the example of Lou, who wished to remain anonymous, and her two children. They began to struggle financially after she separated from her partner a couple of years ago. Lou works full time as a complex needs carer and has moved into a small flat, but finds keeping up with the rent every month a struggle.

"I couldn't afford to buy my son a proper birthday present this year," she said. "I felt awful about it, but I don't think you should hide everything from your children. You don't want to expose them to too much, but at the same time if you simply can't afford things, you have to explain that to them.

"I'm working hard, but it still makes me feel like a failure. I recently changed jobs and hit a rough patch when I thought I wouldn't be able to pay the rent. An employer had given me some work and didn't tell me that my hours wouldn't be guaranteed. I lost a chunk of my income all of a sudden and very nearly lost my home. It was really scary.

"There's never a cushion. You'd think if you were working, you'd be able to save a little bit every month, but it's just not a possibility when paying for the basics is so expensive."

9 August 2016

⇨ The above is reprinted with kind permission from *The Guardian*. Please visit www.theguardian. com for further information.

© 2018 Guardian News and Media Limited

Household debt will reach record high in first year of new government, says TUC

⇨ Unsecured debt per household will pass pre-crisis peak this year, and exceed £15,000 by 2020

⇨ Low wage, low investment model is pushing the economy into the danger zone, says TUC

⇨ Next government must deliver plan to address living standards crisis

The TUC is today (Thursday) publishing new analysis of household debt, which finds that unsecured debt per household will reach a record high of £13,900 this year.

Unsecured debt per household was £13,200 in 2016 – the highest figure since the financial crisis, and only marginally below the peak of £13,300 in 2007.

The TUC analysis also finds that unsecured debt per household is set to exceed £15,000 before the end of the next parliament (all figures are in 2016 prices).

The rise in household debt reflects the UK's ongoing living standards crisis, says the TUC. Wages in the UK are still worth around £20 per week less than before the financial crisis a decade ago. And official figures from the ONS show that real wages are now falling again.

The TUC believes the growth in household debt should concern all the political parties. The next government will inherit an economy that is heavily reliant on household spending to maintain growth, but in which debt per household is higher than before the financial crisis.

County Court debt judgements against consumers have risen 35% in England and Wales, and the Bank of England is investigating concerns about unsecured lending to households.

TUC General Secretary Frances O'Grady said: "The surge in household debt is putting the economy in the danger zone.

"We've got this problem because wages haven't recovered. Credit cards and payday loans are helping to prop up household spending for now, but millions of families are running on empty.

"The next government must act urgently to deliver the higher wages Britain needs for sustainable growth. They must boost the minimum wage, and end pay restrictions for public servants like nurses, firefighters and midwives.

"A lot more government support is needed for the parts of Britain where well-paid jobs are in short supply. Communities that lack good jobs today could thrive tomorrow if they get proper investment in training, transport links, broadband and decent housing."

1. The analysis is based on debt data from the Office for National Statistics, and the most recent economic forecast by the Office for Budget Responsibility.

2. All figures are in 2016 prices.

3. Unsecured household debt is defined as the total stock of loans to households excluding lending secured on dwellings – i.e. mortgage debt is not included; but debts like credit cards, store cards, pay day loans, bank loans, student loans and car loans are included.

4. Outturn figures are derived from the balance sheet for the household sector published by the ONS in *UK Economic Accounts*, Table 6.1.9. Unsecured credit is calculated as total loans (NNRE) excluding long-term loans secured on dwellings (NNRP).

5. The projection over 2017–2021 is based on Office for Budget Responsibility figures for unsecured loans, from Table 1.11 of the November 2016 *Economic and Fiscal Outlook: Economy* (supplementary tables).

6. An adjustment is made for the National Accounts entries that are not included in the calculation for the historic figures: 'debt securities', NNQC; 'pensions schemes', M9VU; 'financial derivatives and employee stock options', MMY9; and 'other accounts payable', NNSQ.

7. The amount of unsecured debt per household is an average taken across all UK households. As some households will not have any unsecured debt, the typical debt of an indebted household will be higher still.

8. While student loans and car loans are significant factors in the growth of unsecured household debt, the TUC believes there should be no complacency about their contribution. They both add to the problem of cash-constrained households saddled with large debts to service each month. And this reduces demand and spending elsewhere in the economy where growth is needed.

25 May 2017

⇨ The above is reprinted with kind permission from The TUC. Please visit www.tuc.org.uk for further information.

© 2018 Trades Union Congress

Record 60 per cent of Britons in poverty live in working families, study shows

The risk of poverty for adults in working households has increased by 27 per cent over the past decade, researchers found.

More than half of Britons living below the poverty line are in a household where someone is in work, a study has found,

Despite Theresa May's recent saying that she believed that work was "the best route out of poverty", researchers at Cardiff University found a record 60 per cent of those in poverty live in a household where someone is in employment.

They also found that the risk of poverty for adults in working households had increased by more than a quarter (27 per cent) over the past decade.

The findings indicate that it is the number of workers in a household and not low pay, that is the primary determinant of in-work poverty, the researchers said.

It comes after Theresa May said in April that she believed work was "the best route out of poverty", adding: "We need a system that does provide support for those who need it, but I think we do need to incentivise people to get into the workplace."

The report states that working families are on average, better off than those without a working member, but adds that "people are not averages and work fails to lift a substantial number of families above the poverty line".

Dr Rod Hick from Cardiff University, who led the research, said: "There has been a lot of discussion recently about how increasing the minimum wage can help to reduce poverty.

"However, what our report finds is that less than half of adults experiencing in-work poverty have a low-paid worker in their household, and most low-paid workers live in non-poor households.

"Low pay is one of the reasons why in-work poverty occurs, but it's not the only reason, and indeed, it is a secondary factor behind the amount of work conducted by household members."

While the study found that tax credits, which supplement income for people on low wages, have been effective in reducing in-work poverty over the past decade, it highlighted that they are received by less than half of working poor households – indicating that their efficacy is over-estimated.

The report also found the rise in in-work poverty has been concentrated among social housing tenants and those in the private rented sector, who have been hit by a combination of rising rents and caps on housing benefit, suggesting housing is an important factor that is overlooked.

"Our research finds that housing costs are becoming an increasingly important factor in determining poverty rates amongst working families," Dr Hick added.

"If policy does not do more to tackle rising housing costs directly, then it seems likely that these will eat up gains made elsewhere – for example, in terms of the planned increases in the minimum wage."

In light of the findings, the report recommends that more should be done to support families with children to enable them to take up additional paid employment through ensuring childcare is available and affordable.

It also suggests reversing cuts to tax credits to ensure that low income working families are supported, as well as tackling the high housing costs experienced by families.

"Tackling in-work poverty requires re-thinking our approach: it's about improving the circumstances of the whole household, not just those of an individual worker, and promoting employment is key," Dr Hick said.

The researchers analysed data from the *Households below average income* report for 2014–15, which is the most recent available.

Then they compared it with reports from 2004–5, 2007–8 and 2010–11. They also looked at Understanding Society, a survey of about 40,000 UK households.

23 May 2017

⇨ The above is reprinted with kind permission from *The Independent*. Please visit www.independent. co.uk for further information.

© independent.co.uk 2018

Is there something special about family meals?

Exploring how family meal habits relate to young children's diets.

Key points

⇨ Children who eat a main meal at a regular time, rather than snack throughout the day, have healthier diets.

⇨ Eating the same food as parents is linked to better dietary quality in children. This may be because 'child-friendly' alternatives to adult food are likely to be nutritionally inferior.

⇨ Eating at the same time as the rest of the family or eating with parents, are not significantly associated with diet.

⇨ Children who eat their meal in a living-room or bedroom are more likely to have poor diets than those who eat in the kitchen or a dining space.

⇨ In families where mothers describe mealtimes as enjoyable or as opportunities to talk, children are less likely to have poorer diets.

⇨ Higher maternal educational achievement is linked to better diets in children. It is likely that some of the eating habits which predict better diet simply reflect the affluence and socio-economic background of families.

Some 35% of teenagers in Scotland are overweight or obese, more than anywhere else in Europe (IASO data for 2012). This points to an urgent need to improve children's diets. Child nutrition policy in Scotland has primarily focused on infants or on school-aged children. Policy recommendations regarding the nutrition of toddlers (2–5 years) are much less developed. Also, existing recommendations on food consumption limits (e.g. two grams of salt for children up to three years old) and food consumption targets (e.g. five-a-day for children aged five and over) do not necessarily reflect the ways parents and families think of food. Research suggests that preparing family meals encourages better diets in children, and may be a good way to address and improve the nutrition of toddlers. This briefing outlines some key findings of a research project which explored this by asking if and why family meals promote better eating habits in children under five years of age.

The study

Research has shown that family meals are generally linked to positive nutritional outcomes. Yet it is unclear what it is about the family meal and eating together which makes it so beneficial to children. This study has specifically addressed this issue exploring whether the quality of children's diets is linked to how, when, where, and with whom children eat. Family characteristics known to be associated with diet, such as socio-demographic status, maternal education and family composition, were controlled in the analysis to adjust for the effect that these have on both dietary quality and meal habits.

This project presents a very Scottish picture. Most existing evidence of children's diets is based on US samples, and cannot account for the cultural and policy context of the UK and Scotland. Using data from the Growing Up in Scotland (GUS) study (www.growingupinscotland.org.uk), information on diet and meal habits from 2,332 children aged four years and ten months was analysed. This study has deliberately focused on pre-school children, as most existing evidence is based on older children, by which time eating habits are already well established. The analysis for this project focused on the quality of children's diets. To capture children's dietary quality, a standardised scale was constructed from nine questions which measured how often children ate fruit, vegetables, crisps, sweets, fizzy drinks, whether children had a varied diet, and whether children snack between meals. The analysis then used this scale to explore the relationship between the quality of children's diets and:

⇨ meal occurrence

⇨ meal habits

⇨ meal enjoyment and

⇨ family characteristics.

Factors significantly associated with healthier diets

What helps

⇨ Eating a main meal

⇨ Not snacking much

⇨ Having regular meal times

⇨ Eating the same food as parents

⇨ Eating in a dining-designated space

⇨ Where meals are considered as enjoyable and a 'time to talk to each other'

- ⇨ Being the first-born child
- ⇨ A mother with more formal education.

What is not significant

- ⇨ Eating with the rest of the family or at the same time as parents
- ⇨ If meal times are described as rushed
- ⇨ Child's gender
- ⇨ Mother's age, employment status or ethnic background
- ⇨ Being a couple- or single-parent household.

Discussion

Children from less advantaged backgrounds have poorer diets, consistent with previous research in this area. There has been considerably less work which has looked at meal enjoyment and dietary quality. This research suggests that families which felt that meal times offer an opportunity for quality time had children with healthier diets. However, it is difficult to assess whether enjoying meal times does, in itself, lead to a healthier diet, since what children eat may be equally significant in predicting meal enjoyment.

Family meal habits appeared to be very important in explaining children's diets, independently of the effect that family socio-demographic characteristics had on diet. Perhaps questions on meal habits are reflecting distinctions among social groups which are not appropriately reflected in the family characteristics controlled for in the analysis. It could be that irregular meal schedules or not eating in a dining-space are not, in themselves, detrimental to health but these meal habits traditionally go hand in hand with other family characteristics which predict poorer eating habits. Also, it could be that the dietary preferences of children, influenced by factors not controlled for in the models (e.g. children's personalities, innate food preferences) subsequently influence how families eat.

If we assume that the family characteristics controlled for in the model adequately capture the differences in family socioeconomic circumstances, it would be safe to conclude that meals which are more structured and more enjoyable, and particularly meals where children and parents eat the same foods, predict better and healthier diets in children. A variety of factors may explain why these meal habits are important. The detrimental effects of frequent snacking could be related to the fact that snacks often involve nutritionally poor foods compared to meals. It could also be that frequent snacking, fewer family meals and less regular meal times, are indicative of poor parental control and a lack of routine and structure in disciplining children. Eating in a room not traditionally associated with the consumption of a meal, such as the living room or a bedroom was linked to poorer dietary quality, but this could be reflective of material poverty, such as living in smaller homes with no designated dining space. It could also be that children who eat in nonmeal-specific spaces are simultaneously exposed to the TV (e.g. in a living room or bedroom), which in itself is associated with poorer diets in children.

Research with older children has generally found that regularly eating meals together as a family is linked to more nutritious diets, but eating the same food as parents seems to be the aspect of family meal habits most strongly linked with children's dietary quality in this study. In fact, the less often children ate the same food as parents, the poorer their diets were. The subtle difference in these two findings may simply reflect that children eating with adults are more likely to be eating 'adult' foods, rather than poorer child-friendly alternatives. This is supported by research which has found that children are more likely to eat certain foods if their parents eat them as well.

Children are nutritionally better-off by eating the same food as parents, and this holds independently of whether children eat meals together with parents or not. When children refuse to eat adult food during the family meal, it is a common coping strategy for parents to create separate and different child-friendly food alternatives often of inferior nutritional value to the family meal. This seems to be a wide spread phenomenon, also reflected via 'child-menus' offered at restaurants which are typically of poorer nutritional value than 'adult' equivalents. It is important to stress that children appear to be better-off, from a nutritional point of view, by being encouraged to eat what parents eat.

Recommendations

- ⇨ Public health policies and research need to recognise how eating patterns are embedded within broader family habits and beliefs.
- ⇨ Public health policy needs to address the developments in eating habits of young children and their families during the crucial early-years period. This would prevent unhealthy eating habits from developing, an easier and more efficient approach than changing food preferences which have become well engrained.
- ⇨ Initiatives such as the *Nutritional Guidance for Early Years: Food choices for children aged 1-5 years* document, will regulate food offered to toddlers in care settings. More thought is needed to address the diets of toddlers within the context of family life.
- ⇨ It is unrealistic to assume that parents can act as dieticians and monitor various quantitative nutritional targets with mathematical precision. Encouraging and enabling parents to make healthier choices for themselves, and to feed children the same foods they themselves eat, may be a simpler and more applicable public health message.
- ⇨ The above is reprinted with kind permission from Centre for Research on Families and Relationships. Please visit www. era.lib.ed.ac.uk for further information.

© 2018 Centre for Research on Families and Relationships

Children want parents to "stop sharing their photos online and put phones down"

Children also wanted their parents to be more engaged during conversations.

By Kashmira Gander

"Stop using your phone when I'm talking to you" may sound like what an angry parent would say to a child, but it is in fact a rule that young people wish to impose on their families, a new study has found.

US researchers surveyed 249 families with children between the ages of ten to 17 about how technology use was restricted in their households.

The children were also asked which rules they wished they could impose on their parents. Researchers found there were seven common themes.

Parents shouldn't share information, including photos, online about their children without their explicit permission, the participants also said.

Children also wanted their parents to be more present and stop using technology during conversatons, and use devices in moderation.

An apparent fear for safety among children was also highlighted, as they asked parents to stop texting while they were driving or at a traffic light.

They agreed that parents should establish and enforce rules to protect them, but said that children should make their own decisions and not be interfered with after that point.

Children also wished that parents would follow rules which they impose themselves and stop using devices at mealtimes.

However, parents prioritised privacy rules to reduce the risk of children sharing personal information online over concerns their offspring raised.

Sarita Schoenebeck, assistant professor in the University of Michigan's School of Information and co-author of the study said: "Twice as many children as parents expressed concerns about family members oversharing personal information about them on Facebook and other social media without permission.

"Many children said they found that content embarrassing and felt frustrated when their parents continued to do it."

9 March 2016

⇨ The above is reprinted with kind permission from *The Independent*. Please visit www.independent.co.uk for further information.

© independent.co.uk 2018

Parents are fibbing about cooking for their children, exclusive new research reveals

Nearly a fifth of mums and dads are feeling the pressure about feeding their kids.

By Sarah Ann Harris

Parents are lying about what they cook for their children because they feel guilty about their kids' meals, worrying new research reveals today.

Nearly a fifth (18%) of mums and dads have fibbed about what they make for their children's meals, a new study conducted by YouGov for The Huffington Post UK shows.

The exclusive poll, released as part of HuffPost UK's month-long project, Thriving Families, reveals that 43% of parents feel under pressure to cook healthily for their children – and almost one in ten said they lied about what they made because they knew they should be making healthier meals.

Almost 40% also said they felt pushed to be more adventurous with their food choices.

Jamie Oliver, who is guest-editing HuffPost UK for the launch of Thriving Families, said: "The results mean we still have a very long way to go when it comes to inspiring parents to cook better food for their kids.

"The fact that 18% of parents admit to telling fibs about what they feed their children suggests that there are many parents who know they should be cooking more nutritious meals but, for whatever reason, feel that they can't," Oliver continued.

"More concerning still, is that only 21% of parents are cooking from scratch every day, which means that the majority of kids are still eating processed food. When you read figures like this, it's hardly a surprise. I believe it's a parent or guardian's duty to help teach their kids about food."

The research found that over a fifth of parents (23%) said that the ever-changing cost of food was part of the problem when it came to preparing healthy food.

According to Office for National Statistics (ONS) data the average UK household spends £58.80 on food and non-alcoholic drinks. This is compared with an average of £74.80 on transport and £68.80 on recreation and culture.

But lack of time is also a big problem for many parents.

On average, nearly a third of those surveyed (32%) said that not having enough time prevented them from making healthy meals for their children. Among parents aged between 35 and 44, this rose to 40% – something which could be attributable to struggling to find a work-life balance.

Registered nutritionist Charlotte Stirling-Reed told HuffPost UK that time is a "really common" issue for families.

She said: "We live in a very different society today and, with both parents often out at work and little time at home, finding time for meals and food prep can be tough.

"However, food is such an important and central part of our lives and I always encourage people to try to dedicate just a little more time to nutrition and lifestyle – which can support both our emotional and physical health.

"With clever planning, budgeting and organisation, healthy meals are achievable for most people. There are some fantastic recipes out there with a mix of complexities and some of which are very quick to create too."

Stirling-Reed said she felt families needed more support, adding that this could help avoid embarrassment for parents and the feeling they may need to lie about what they are cooking.

"This shows perhaps that many parents are in fact aware about what foods we should and shouldn't be giving to children," she said.

"I feel parents need more support and that we also need a collaborative approach from all sectors – government, health care, policy makers, industry – in order to help change behaviours.

"This can help ensure that parents don't have to feel guilty or embarrassed about what they feed their children, and, importantly, that the diet of our next generation improves at the same time," Stirling-Reed added.

Convenience is also an issue, with just a fifth (21%) of parents cooking meals from scratch every day, and another fifth (20%) only cooking from scratch once a week or less.

The 2016 *Modern Families Index* showed that around 75% of parents relied on ready meals because of work-related time constraints at least occasionally and in some cases more often.

As well as ready meals, the rise of the takeaway culture is also likely to have contributed to this – and no surprise when the number of takeaway outlets rose by 45% between 1990 and 2008. The increase was greatest in areas that had the highest level of deprivation, according to a 2015 University of Cambridge study.

With the increasing popularity of food delivery services and apps, takeaway food is more accessible than ever before.

Almost a third (29%) of parents also said that fussy eating was another obstacle to making their children healthy meals.

15 July 2017

⇨ The above is reprinted with kind permission from *The Huffington Post*. Please visit www.huffingtonpost.co.uk for further information.

© 2018 AOL (UK) Limited

Helicopter or lawnmower? Modern parenting styles can get in the way of raising well-balanced children

An article from The Conversation.

THE CONVERSATION

By Amy Brown, Associate Professor of Child Public Health, Swansea University

When many middle-aged people think back to their childhood, they remember roaming the streets with their friends during long, hot summers. Our parents threw us out the door in the morning and instructed us not to come back until dinnertime. Often in charge of younger siblings, we strayed further than we should have, got into trouble and, by the end of the summer, had a collection of triumphs, scars and memories for life.

But surely such memories are just nostalgia? The bit about the sun always shining probably is. Yet one thing is certain – the level of parental involvement and supervision in the 1970s was not a tenth of what is expected today. Fast forward to 2014 and a woman was arrested for allowing her nine-year-old to play in the park while she worked.

So what impact do increasing levels of parental involvement have on children? Let's take a look at the evidence.

A recent survey of children aged eight to 12 found that indoor play is now the norm, a third have never splashed in a puddle and the distance children are allowed to play from home has shrunk by 90% since 1970.

Parenting hasn't only changed in terms of what is considered safe for children. Parents now worry more about the impact of their parenting on their children, feeling pressured to provide a stream of stimulating activities in a way that would have once seemed absurd. This has led to the emergence of two types of related parenting styles: the 'helicopter' and the 'lawnmower'.

Helicopter parents, as the name suggests, spend a lot of time hovering. They always stay close to their children, ready to swoop in and direct, help or protect (usually before it is needed). Lawnmower parents are one step ahead of their children, smoothing their path and making sure nothing gets in their way. Common tactics of both include interfering significantly with their grown-up children's lives, such as complaining to employers when their children don't get a job.

But does enabling a childhood free from stress really help them in the long term? And what happens when children never have to get themselves out of tricky situations?

Not rocket science

As with anything, there is a middle ground. It doesn't take a rocket scientist to realise that providing children with opportunities and support helps them to gain experiences, confidence and networks that they wouldn't be offered in more adverse settings. But there is an important line between supporting children and wrapping them in gold-plated cotton wool.

Allowing children freedom to take appropriate risks through outdoor play is essential for their development. Risky play does not mean placing children in grave danger, but instead allowing them to be children – climbing, jumping from heights and hanging upside down are good examples. Risky play allows children to test limits and solve problems. And, yes, this includes learning what happens when they overstretch themselves and fall.

But what about the abduction risk? Won't children who are allowed outside unsupervised be kidnapped? Highly unlikely. Despite headlines suggesting otherwise, the risk of child abduction has not increased from approximately a 0.0005% chance since data was first collected in the 1970s.

And children are actually far more likely to be abducted by someone they know (even a parent) than the feared stranger lurking in the shadows.

Aside from risk, constantly intervening and providing opportunities for children is not good for their development. We may have forgotten it in our hot, hazy memories, but it is normal – and beneficial – for children to be bored. Boredom enhances creativity and problem solving, whereas constant input dulls imagination – even if that includes creative classes.

Continually hovering and doing things for children may also backfire. Children whose parents frequently intervene are more likely to experience anxiety. Although the link is not necessarily causal, being constantly rescued is likely to reduce your confidence. Meanwhile, when children play alone they meet challenges – and learn to solve problems, honing their creativity skills in the process.

These early interactions may also have long-term consequences. Research with college students has found that the higher the degree of parental 'helicoptering', the greater the risk of student depression and anxiety. On the flip side, those students who are used to their parents enabling everything, are more likely to display traits of narcissism and entitlement. Anxiety is not good, but neither is overconfidence and an expectation that life should be easy.

Having said all of that, parental involvement, particularly from warm, loving but firm parents, is of course beneficial. While having confidence in their own abilities may contribute to a child's sense of security, so will having supportive parents. And let's not forget that although abductions may not have risen, the amount of traffic has, and freedom and risks need to be appropriate.

Striking the right balance may seem more complicated than it has to be.

Over 50 years ago, paediatrician and psychoanalyst Donald Woods Winnicott introduced the concept of 'good enough parenting'. He showed that parents who were loving and provided a stimulating environment – but also set boundaries and didn't stress about doing enough – had children with the best outcomes.

Perhaps Winnicott was blinded by nostalgia thinking back to long, hot summers. But many experts today still believe it's a strategy that makes a lot of sense for raising secure and independent children.

19 July 2017

⇨ The above is reprinted with kind permission from *The Conversation*. Please visit www.theconversation.com for further information.

© 2010-2018 The Conversation Trust (UK)

It's okay, it's just my parents.

Home life and age of puberty

"Girls who live in a happy and stable family mature later and are less likely to develop mood disorders, substance abuse and certain cancers," reports *The Daily Telegraph* today. The newspaper reports that in homes with fewer marriage problems and depression, girls go through puberty later.

This story is based on research using data collected during the children's preschool and early school years. The study found a link between the age at which girls develop secondary sexual characteristics and the parental support they receive during their preschool years. The study is a reliable one; however, a stable family life is just one of many factors that are likely to influence the age of a girl's first period, and one of these that the study may not have accounted for, is genetics. In addition, the study did not investigate how the timing of puberty is linked to any health-related issues later in life.

Where did the story come from?

Bruce Ellis and Marilyn Essex of the University of Arizona and the University of Wisconsin carried out this research. The study was funded by grants from the National Institute of Mental Health and the MacArthur Foundation Research Network on Psychopathology and Development. It was published in the peer-reviewed medical journal: *Child Development*.

What kind of scientific study was this?

The study is a prospective cohort study which uses a representative subset of data from children who were included in a bigger study – the Wisconsin Study of Families and Work (WSFW). In the WSFW, pregnant women were enrolled and data were collected, using questionnaires and interviews, about them and their children throughout the child's infancy and early schooling. For this publication, the researchers were interested in seeing whether family environment influenced 'adrenarche' in boys and girls in Grade 1 (age about 6.8 to 7.8 years). Adrenarche is the time when the adrenal glands mature and begin to function. It takes place before puberty, usually at ages six to eight years in both boys and girls.

The researchers were also interested in whether family environment had any effect on secondary sexual characteristics in girls who were aged about 10.5 to 11.9 years (Grade 5). They had information available on a range of different characteristics of these families, including the mothers' age when her periods started, socioeconomic status, parents' reports of marital conflict/depression, measures of parental supportiveness, child's height and weight and so on. Adrenarche was determined in the children by testing for the presence of a hormone found in the saliva. Secondary sexual characteristics in girls were determined using questionnaires to mothers and girls that rated appearance of pubic hair and the breast development stage. Using statistical methods, the researchers determined which of the family factors had an effect on whether the child had reached adrenarche by Grade 1 or whether there were signs of secondary sexual characteristics by Grade 5. They used complex mathematical methods to explore some of these relationships further.

What were the results of the study?

The researchers found that the children who had reached adrenarche by Grade 1 were more likely to be from families where 'parental supportiveness' was lower during preschool years. They were also more likely to be from families where father-reported marital conflict/depression was high, though this didn't seem to be the case when they looked at the mothers' reporting of marital conflict/depression. They found that socioeconomic status had no effect on adrenarche.

In terms of secondary sexual characteristics in girls, they found that development was delayed in families where there was high parental supportiveness in preschool and a higher socioeconomic status. Overall, they found that later sexual development in girls was predicted by a later age at mothers' first period, higher socioeconomic status, greater mother-based parental support and higher body mass index (BMI).

What interpretations did the researchers draw from these results?

The researchers conclude that the results of their study support a theory – 'psychosocial acceleration theory' – which predicts that the higher the quality of parenting in the preschool years, the slower the rate of sexual maturity (shown by lower rates of adrenarche in boys and girls in Grade 1 and less development of secondary sexual characteristics in girls in Grade 5). They say that their findings about marital conflict/depression are not helpful and "further cloud the already contradictory literature" on whether family conflict accelerates puberty.

What does the NHS Knowledge Service make of this study?

There are several points to keep in mind:

⇨ The 'model' that the researchers developed was able to show that the later age of sexual development for girls was linked to mothers' age at first period, BMI, parental supportiveness, marital conflict/depression and socioeconomic status. However, the researchers say that these factors accounted for only 25% of the variation in sexual maturity. There are other factors involved that the researchers have not investigated. One of the most important factors that may not have been fully addressed is genetics. The researchers say that although they tried to consider this by looking at mothers' age at first period, they "cannot be certain by any means that the effects of biological inheritance have been fully accounted for".

⇨ As the researchers highlight, the children in their study were all Caucasians. No information is available then about other ethnicities. Both family environment and the timing of puberty are known to vary between ethnic groups.

⇨ There were different parts to the study's results depending on how the researchers analysed the data. They do not, however, find any link between marital conflict/depression and the development of secondary sexual characteristics in girls. The report in the newspapers may suggest that a link was found, but this is not the case. The researchers did find that mothers' reports of marital conflict/depression were linked to BMI and to measures of parental supportiveness. This shows that there are complex interactions going on between the characteristics.

As the authors acknowledge, there are clearly many factors that may predict or even determine the timing of the onset of puberty. Parental supportiveness seems an essential in order to bring up healthy young children and it should be promoted without any need to resort to complex modelling theories.

Sir Muir Gray adds...

Inequality is bad for your heath and the effects start early, even before birth, never mind at puberty. Although most people think of money when inequality is mentioned, inequality in family stability is another aspect that can have adverse effects.

15 November 2017

⇨ The above is reprinted with kind permission from NHS Choices. Please visit www.nhs.uk for further information.

© NHS Choices 2018

Is it illegal to smack children in the UK?

Smacking may make parenting harder in the long run, not easier.

By Tamsin Kelly

What's the current law on smacking children in the UK?

It is legal for a parent or carer to smack their own child in England, Wales and Northern Ireland when it amounts to 'reasonable punishment', as laid down in section 58 of the Children Act 2004.

But whether a smack can be judged reasonable punishment will depend on the age of the child and the force involved in smacking. Parents have the right to choose to discipline their children with a smack, but there is a fine line between what some parents would regard as 'reasonable' (and therefore a defence in law) and assault, which is a criminal offence.

Hitting a child in a way which causes wounding, actual bodily harm, grievous bodily harm or child cruelty are all illegal. A parent could be charged with common assault if a child is left with any of these injuries:

⇨ Scratches

⇨ Abrasions

⇨ Minor bruising

⇨ Swellings

⇨ Reddening of the skin

⇨ Superficial cuts

⇨ A black eye.

For even more serious injuries – cuts, multiple bruising, fractures, broken bones, broken teeth or loss of consciousness – a parent could be charged with actual bodily harm.

Smacking children is set to be banned in Scotland, the Scottish Government confirmed on Thursday 19 October. The country will be the first part of the UK to make the physical punishment of children illegal.

Wales is set to be the next country to make smacking illegal. On Universal Children's Day [20 November] the Welsh Minister for Children, Huw Irranca-Davies, said: "It can no longer be acceptable in a modern and progressive society for children to be physically punished.

"It is right that as a government, we take action to protect children and support parents to use positive and effective alternatives to physical punishment."

What about teachers and caregivers?

It is against the law for teachers, nursery workers and child care workers to smack children – and definitely no rulers or canes! However, they are allowed to use 'reasonable force' to restrain a child.

And, just to complicate the legal/illegal smacking grey areas, it is legal for parents employing nannies, au pairs and childminders privately to give them permission to smack the children in their care.

Is smacking illegal in other countries?

Globally, 52 countries have made the physical punishment of children illegal. Sweden was the first in 1979 and France the most recent country with its ban in 2017. The Republic of Ireland banned smacking in 2015.

In Europe, only four countries – Italy, Switzerland, the Czech Republic and the UK – continue to allow the 'reasonable punishment' of children.

In 2015 the UN issued a public rebuke to the UK nations for not complying with its Convention on the Rights of the Child and stated that corporal punishment should not be allowed in "all settings including the home" and that the UK should "encourage non-violent forms of discipline instead".

So why isn't smacking banned in the UK?

It's a controversial subject. The Scottish Government is currently consulting on a ban and the Welsh Government plans to do the same in the next 12 months. Meanwhile the debate rolls on...

What are the arguments for and against smacking?

Those who support the right to smack their own children say it works as a way of chastising children and preventing repeated bad behaviour, that it never did them any harm as children and that the 'nanny state' should not intervene in what happens within their homes or criminalise parents.

Those who oppose smacking say that it is an outdated discipline method that has no place in a civilised society. They say that smacking children simply does not work and is an abuse of vulnerable children by adults. They point out the absurdity of criminalising smoking in a car with a child, but allowing smacking to continue.

An NSPCC spokesperson told HuffPost UK: "Parents are often under pressure but the NSPCC believes that smacking is not the best way to resolve problems or improve behaviour.

"Hitting children only teaches them to use violence. If you were trying to convince an adult not to do something you wouldn't hit them, so why would you do that to a child?"

Instead the NSPCC and many child experts promote positive parenting, using positive ways to bring up children with praise, repetition, clear boundaries and expectations and explanation. The children's charity says: "Smacking can hurt children's feelings - making them resentful and angry and damaging the relationship between parent and child. This makes parenting and discipline harder in the long run, not easier. Smacking can get out of control.

"This also comes back to being a role model. If you smack your child, they may think this is acceptable behaviour

and treat other people in the same way. Children may avoid being smacked by lying or hiding how they feel. And they may become withdrawn – not developing independence.

"When you give out love, you get it back. When you give out harsh punishment – screaming, yelling or hitting – this means you are eventually likely to get anger and resentment back."

Parents' suggestions of alternative ways to improve children's behaviour, without resorting to smacks

"Children care what parents think. They want to make us happy and proud. I praise my kids when they act responsibly and unselfishly and are a pleasure to be around. I've never needed to smack. A stern word, a disapproving frown can speak volumes when I'm disappointed or expected better."

Dominique

"Smacking doesn't work. It's a loss of control. The only time I tried to smack my daughter she was about two - and she smacked me straight back, both of us shouting and then crying. We used the naughty step idea as a time out to think about being nicer and calm things down."

Siobhan

"Clear boundaries and expectations, praise them when they're good, tell them off when they're naughty – and hugs. It's not rocket science."

Hugh

"My dad smacked me with a slipper. I hated the humiliation of being 12, 13 and still being smacked. I've never raised a hand to my five children. I wanted to earn their love and respect. I celebrate the good behaviour and ignore the bad. That seems to work."

Jack

"My job as a parent is to bring my child up to be a kind member of our civilised society. We have to explain right from wrong; I don't show her right by doing wrong and smacking her. I want to be a better role model than that. There are times when I feel overwhelmed but then I take myself away for a few minutes."

Laura

23 November 2017

⇨ The above is reprinted with kind permission from *The Huffington Post*. Please visit www. huffingtonpost.co.uk for further information.

© 2018 AOL (UK) Limited

Kinship carers: soaring number of children brought up by relatives other than parents

Of 150,000 children brought up by grandparents, siblings or other relatives, three-quarters are in deprived households.

Emily Dugan, Social Affairs Editor

The proportion of children being brought up by grandparents, siblings or other more distant relatives has risen dramatically over the past decade, research has found.

Around 150,000 English children are growing up in a home with relatives other than their parents, according to an analysis of census figures by the University of Bristol. More than three-quarters of these children are in deprived households, raising questions about the level of support available to 'kinship' carers.

Between 2001 and 2011 the number of children looked after by family members other than parents rose by seven per cent, far exceeding the two per cent growth in the child population as a whole. The number of children in kinship care is likely to have increased further following the recent fall in the number of children deemed eligible for adoption.

76%
The proportion of kinship children living in a deprived household

The impact on adoption of a series of rulings in the family courts in favour of finding alternative relatives was revealed in *The Independent* earlier this year. The judgments have made local authorities and judges cautious about proceeding with adoption unless kinship care has been explored at length.

Poverty is prevalent among children in kinship families, the research revealed, with 76 per cent living in a deprived household. Compared with children growing up with at least one parent,

those raised by kinship carers were also found to be nearly twice as likely to have long-term health problems or disabilities.

Dinithi Wijedasa, the study's lead author from the University of Bristol's Hadley Centre for Foster and Adoption Studies, said: "As well as showing a significant increase in the number of kinship care households, the findings highlight that children growing up in the care of relatives face significant poverty and deprivation compared with children growing up with at least one parent.

"Children in kinship care are also more likely to have a disability or higher levels of long-term health problems. Given that a large majority of these children and their families will be not known to the local authorities, it is imperative that measures are taken to enable them to receive adequate support."

Black children are more likely than any other group to be looked after by a relative other than their parents, the research found. One in every 37 black children is brought up by kinship carers, compared with just one in 83 white children.

Although often stepping in during a moment of family crisis, similar to adoptive parents, kinship carers receive less support than them, despite often being worse off financially. Research from Family Rights Group, also published today, found that almost half of kinship carers have had to give up work permanently to care for a kin child and a further 18 per cent had to stop working temporarily. Almost two-thirds receive child tax credit and 34 per cent receive housing benefit.

Cathy Ashley, chief executive of Family Rights Group, said: "The number of children living in kinship care is increasing, and they are overwhelmingly affected by poverty… We call on the Government to take action to introduce a period of paid leave for kinship carers, similar to adoption leave, to enable the children to settle in without the carers being forced to give up work."

Grandparents are the most common main carer, accounting for 51 per cent of the kinship children, while just under a quarter are raised by siblings. The remainder are brought up by another relative.

Lucy Peake, chief executive of Grandparents Plus, said: "It is shocking that such a high proportion of children growing up in the care of a grandparent or other family member experience poverty and deprivation… The Government's proposals to cut child tax credits and reform welfare benefits threaten to make their situation even worse."

My Story: I was raised by my grandparents

Brad Smith, 16, from Worcester, has been raised by his grandparents on his mother's side.

My mum had me quite young, when she was 16. I don't really see her at all and I don't know my dad.

I like living with my grandparents. Everyone likes my nan. She's a motherly figure to me. My nan does find it harder than if she was my mum because she is older – she's 50 and she gets tired quite quickly.

We do argue a bit but I don't know what it would be like being raised by mum instead of my nan because I don't see her.

My nan is quite protective but lets me get on with things. She'll point stuff out I should and shouldn't do but lets me find out things for myself. All my mates like her, so I'm guessing that means she's a good parent.

My granddad and I do argue – I think it's the age difference because things were different in his day. I just don't see eye to eye with him sometimes.

My nan has taught me empathy and to treat people how you want to be treated.

My friends respect what my grandparents are doing. They treat me well. I think the world of my nan for what she's supported me through.

She's set up a group called Kinship Carers – we run youth groups for children going through similar things. It's for young kids right up until my age. It gives me the opportunity to support other kids going through these things, we play football and do all sorts of activities.

12 October 2015

⇨ The above is reprinted with kind permission from *The Independent*. Please visit www.independent for further information.

© independent.co.uk 2018

School holidays leave three million children at risk of hunger, report says

Cross-party group of MPs and peers cites evidence of children existing on diets of crisps when school canteens are shut.

By Patrick Butler, Social Policy Editor

Up to three million children risk going hungry during the school holidays, leaving them vulnerable to malnutrition and undermining their education and life chances, a cross-party group of MPs and peers has warned.

Its report cited evidence of children existing on holiday diets of crisps, hungry youngsters unable to take part in a football tournament because "their bodies simply gave up", and others surviving on stodgy, unhealthy diets "bought to fill hungry stomachs".

The report said those at risk of hunger over the summer include more than one million children who receive free school meals during term time, and two million more with working parents who are still in poverty.

"The evidence presented in this report is staggering. It shows us that not only are there children in this country who are exposed to hunger when they are not at school, but also that this exposure risks damaging their prospects of gaining a good education and living a healthy life," the group's chair, Frank Field MP, said.

The group also said that ministers should channel £41.5 million raised as part of the planned tax on sugary drinks to help each UK council set up support schemes with local churches and charities aimed at feeding hungry children when school canteens are shut.

The all-party parliamentary group (APPG) on hunger found there was a "deeply troubling" impact on children who had gone hungry over the holidays and returned to class "malnourished, sluggish and dreary".

It said the evidence it had received indicated that those children "start the new term several weeks, if not months, intellectually behind their more fortunate peers who have enjoyed a more wholesome diet and lots of activity".

The report said: "There can be no escape from the reality that in 2017, children in different parts of England, Wales, Scotland and Northern Ireland are arriving back at school hungry and totally unprepared to learn after the holidays.

"We have learnt of one young person who vomited during the holidays because their diet consisted exclusively of packets of crisps. Elsewhere, a group of children taking part in a holiday football tournament had to drop out of the latter stages of the competition, as they had not eaten a meal in the days leading up to the event. Their bodies simply gave up on them."

The positive impact on poorer children who attended free meal and fun projects during the holidays was stark, the report said. They "eat more healthily, undertake more exercise, demonstrate better behaviour, and return to school in a much improved condition than they otherwise would have done in the absence of those projects".

Although the APPG praised voluntary groups which had set up networks of holiday food projects across the UK, it said that overall provision was sporadic and piecemeal, and could not be viewed as a sufficient response to the problem.

Some areas had no coverage at all, and large numbers of children were missing out, it said: "A scarcity of funding, a lack of coordination and a heavy reliance on donations limit our country's ability to protect every child from hunger during school holidays." It called on the Government to back a proposed free school meals (provision in school holidays) bill after the general election. "It [the Government] has now had time to take on board the fact that under its stewardship of the fifth richest country in the world, too many children are stalked by hunger," said Field.

He added: "Abolishing hunger during school holidays is beyond the ability of individual community groups and volunteers alone. It needs, above all, a government lead in giving local authorities duties to convene churches, community groups, businesses, schools and public bodies in their area."

24 April 2017

⇨ The above is reprinted with kind permission from *The Guardian*. Please visit www.theguardian. com. for further information.

© 2018 Guardian News and Media Limited

Grandparent Army Report

An extract from an article by The International Longevity Centre.

Executive summary

Grandparents provide immense support to parents and grandchildren in the UK. With the cost of childcare increasing and both single and two-parent families much more likely to be working, this assistance is vital.

They help with financial aid, care-giving, and skills and hobbies.

In this report we've looked more closely at the type of support given and how grandparents feel about providing it.

Close relationships between grandparents and their children and grandchildren are beneficial to all. They must be encouraged and supported, so we have set out some recommendations for government, employers and education providers that would support achieving this. We hope it goes some way to showing the importance of grandparents and how they can be better acknowledged.

This report finds that

⇨ 37% of parents in Ageas's 2016 Grandparent Army Tracker (GAT) Survey rely on financial support from grandparents to help with the cost of taking care of children.

⇨ Of the grandparents in the GAT survey who provide childcare, the most common things they financially contribute towards are toys and hobbies, leisure and recreational activities, holidays and pocket money.

⇨ The price of childcare in the UK has increased in recent years, with the cost of a part time nursery place for a two-year-old increasing by 20% from 2011–2016. This means the support grandparents give to parents is vital.

⇨ 65% of grandparents in the GAT survey provide some form of childcare.

⇨ The median number of hours of care provided by this group is 11.3.

⇨ Grandparents in England who provide care for grandchildren are more likely to still be in work than those who did not provide any care.

⇨ 44% of parents in the GAT survey rely on grandparents for help with their children's activities or teaching them skills.

⇨ 56% of grandparents in England who provide care for grandchildren strongly agree that they are appreciated for their caring.

⇨ 59% of grandparents in the GAT survey who provide care are not aware of the scheme to share parental leave pay with parents.

Grandparents have always played an important role in providing support for families and grandchildren, but changes in family structures, domestic and international migration, childcare policies and labour force participation have all led to this role being reshaped.

How family structures are changing the role grandparents play

The number of women and mothers in work has grown over the last few decades and, as a result, both parents are often working for at least some of the time their children are not in an educational establishment. For example, before a child is old enough to start school, before or after the school day, or during school holidays. As a result, many families rely on grandparents to provide childcare to their children.

Over the same time, there has been a concerted push by government to extend working lives through policies such as raising the state pension age, abolishing the compulsory retirement age and legislating against age discrimination in the workplace.

These measures have been implemented because of the importance of our more mature workers to the UK's overall economic health and to allow everyone to work for as long as they want to. However, as more and more grandparents remain in employment, it means there will be fewer grandparents available to provide care for their grandchildren.

How attitudes and policies towards childcare have changed

As family structures adapt and there is greater reliance on grandparents to provide support, there has been a change in attitudes and policies towards childcare. Historically, children were looked after by a parent (usually the mother), or other family members. But, since the late 1990s, there has been a move towards more formal provisions of childcare as more mothers returned to work.

With the introduction in the late 1990s of free early years education (i.e. the voucher scheme entitling all four-year-olds to a free school place), Sure Start centres and tax credits for childcare costs, formal childcare became both more available and more affordable. However, there remains significant demand and, maybe even expectation, for informal care provided by grandparents.

Other factors impacting grandparental support

Moving from town to town, or county to county can also affect the levels of support grandparents are able to offer their children and grandchildren. There are obvious benefits to living close to family members and the consequences of living considerable distances apart means the frequency and amount of contact and childcare that can be provided is lessened.

The number of people moving from region to region in England and Wales has remained relatively steady since 1975, with 2.85 million residents moving from one local authority to another in England and Wales during 2015.

International migration may have also impacted grandparental support for grandchildren in the UK.

Recent years have seen a record high in net migration figures, with longer-term trends showing an increase in net migration. The majority of migrants to the UK are of working age, which could

indicate there will be more families in the UK who are unable to rely on grandparental support. The number of grandparents living abroad who provide financial support is unknown.

There are also significant numbers of British grandparents who live outside of the UK, although exactly how many have moved from the UK to another country is difficult to define (a result of differences in how each country defines a 'migrant', differences between countries in census collection, and many expats still being registered citizens in the UK). Nevertheless, studies have estimated that in Spain, for example, 53% of the 990,000 UK nationals living there were aged over 50. This indicates there are many grandparents who live abroad.

As a result of these two population trends some interesting and unexpected insights about the nature and provision of grandparental care in the UK today have been identified. A survey commissioned by the Daycare Trust found that 5% of parents had used a grandparent who normally lived abroad as their main form of childcare in the last six months – a surprisingly high figure. They also report that this figure "is only slightly higher among minority ethnic groups", indicating that grandparents who usually live overseas are used as a main source of childcare

by both white UK families and minority ethnic families. In other words, this group of caregivers is likely to be made up of both UK-born grandparents who have retired overseas, and non-UK born grandparents who still live in their country of origin.

In what ways do grandparents provide childcare?

⇨ As the primary source of childcare for pre-school children.

⇨ Before and after school, and during school holidays.

⇨ As an additional source of care, on top of formal childcare.

⇨ As a source of emergency care, for example due to parental illness.

⇨ The above extract is reprinted with kind permission from the International Longevity Centre. Please visit www.ilcuk.ork.uk for further information.

© 2018 International Longevity Centre

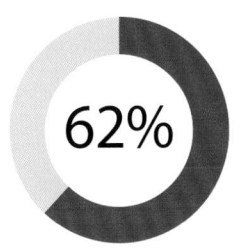

62%

of over 50s in England have a grandchild/grandchildren*

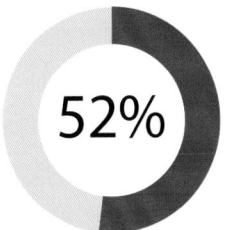

52%

of grandparents in the Ageas survey who provided childcare expect nothing back from their children for caring for their grandchildren†

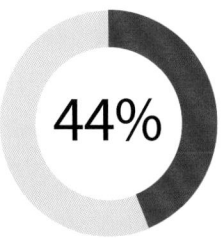

44%

of parents rely on grandparents for help with their children's activities or teaching them skills

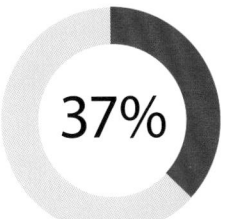

37%

of parents in the Ageas survey rely on financial support from grandparents to help with the cost of taking care of children†

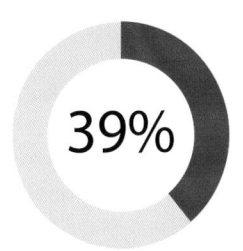

39%

of the grandparents who provide care for their grandchildren are currently in work*

of the grandparents who provided care in the Ageas survey, the median hours of care per week was

11.3

*Source: English longitudinal study of ageing, wave 7). †Source: Ageas survey.

Families with a difference: the reality behind the hype

*Families come in many guises. Some parents are same-sex; others are single by choice. Growing numbers of children are conceived through assistive reproductive technology. What do these developments mean for the parents and children involved? Professor Susan Golombok's book, **Modern Families**, examines 'new family forms' within a context of four decades of empirical research.*

Over the past 40 years the family has altered in ways that few people imagined back in the days of the *Janet and John* reading books in which mummy baked and daddy mowed the lawn. In the 1970s, the 'nuclear' family (heterosexual married couple with genetically related children) was in a clear majority. Advances in assistive reproductive technologies, a rise in numbers of single parent and step families resulting from divorce, and the creation of families by same-sex couples and single people have changed all that. Today 'non-traditional' families outnumber nuclear families in the UK and many other countries.

When it comes to family, everyone has opinions – but they are just opinions. In her new book, *Modern Families: Parents and Children in New Family Forms* (published 12 March 2015), Professor Susan Golombok charts the remarkable changes that have taken place in the context of the empirical research that has sought to answer a series of contested questions. Are children less likely to thrive in families headed by same-sex parents, single mothers by choice or parents who conceived them using assisted reproductive technologies? Will children born to gay fathers through egg donation and surrogacy be less likely to flourish than children conceived by IVF to genetically related heterosexual parents?

Golombok's contribution to family research goes back to 1976 when she responded to an article in the feminist magazine *Spare Rib* by conducting an objective study of the development of children of lesbian mothers. *Spare Rib* had revealed that, both in the UK and US, lesbian mothers in child custody

disputes invariably lost their cases to their ex-husbands. Courts argued that it was not in children's best interests to be raised by lesbian women, not least because their gender development would be skewed. Golombok, and other researchers, have shown in successive studies that boys are no less masculine and girls no less feminine than boys and girls with heterosexual parents.

In 2006 Golombok was appointed director of Cambridge University's Centre for Family Research – a research centre known for its focus on family influences on child development. *Modern Families* brings together for the first time the growing body of research into the wide range of family forms, undertaken not just in the UK but also in the US and around the world. Most strikingly, these studies show, again and again, that it is the quality of relationships that matters most to the well-being of families, not the number, gender, sexual orientation or genetic relatedness of the parents, or whether the child was conceived with the assistance of reproductive technology.

These findings fly in the face of the media hysteria that greeted the birth of the first IVF baby in 1978. Societal attitudes have since moved on. However, deep-seated assumptions of what is 'right and proper' continue to colour notions of what a family 'should' be in order to raise a well-balanced child. Real families are complex. Golombok is careful to be even-handed in her unpacking (family type by family type) of the issues, the arguments and the relevant research in a field that, by virtue of its human intimacy, demands a high level of sensitivity and diplomacy.

She also addresses the fact that research into so emotionally charged

a field is bound to be imperfect. Parents willing to take part in research are more likely to be those who are functioning well than those who struggle. "It is important to study new family forms to find out what they are really like. Otherwise, all we have is speculation and assumption, usually negative, which simply fuel prejudice and discrimination and are harmful to the children involved," she says.

Some findings are counterintuitive, others less so. One of the arguments most famously used against same-sex parenting has been that children may lack models on which to base their own gender identity and behaviour. In a study of play preferences, lesbian mothers chose a mix of masculine and feminine toys but their children chose toys and activities that were highly sex-typed. It seems that parents have little influence over the sex-typed toy and activity preferences of their daughters and sons.

In studies of children born through assisted reproduction, their mothers have consistently been found to show more warmth and emotional involvement, and less parenting stress, than natural conception mothers.

"Contrary to the expectation that parents of children born through assisted reproductive technologies would experience difficulties in parenting, research has found them to be highly committed and involved parents, even in donor-conceived families where one or both parents lack a genetic relationship with their children," says Golombok.

"A key factor in the positive functioning of children in new family forms appears to be that they are very wanted children. Parents in new family forms often struggle to have children against the odds. Many experience years of infertility before becoming parents; others become parents in the face of significant social disapproval; and still others surmount both hurdles in order to have a child."

When surrogacy hit the headlines in 1985 with the case of Kim Cotton, the furore about the payment made to her by the intended parents of the child she was carrying led the UK to outlaw commercial surrogacy. Although attitudes to surrogacy have softened, it remains the most controversial form of assisted reproduction. Studies report that relationships between intended parents and surrogate mothers are generally both enduring and positive. Children born through surrogacy sometimes form relationships with the surrogate's own children.

Modern Families offers a measured appraisal of the broader issues that are likely to prove increasingly salient (and debated) as reproductive technologies offer novel routes to the conception of a healthy child and society's understanding of what constitutes 'family' is increasingly extended. Last month's approval in the UK for the use of a technique called mitochondrial replacement has rekindled accusations of scientists 'playing God'. Perhaps, in time, society will be more accepting of techniques like mitochondrial replacement, developed primarily to avoid a child being born with a devastating medical condition.

Two generations ago, same-sex parenting was widely vilified as 'against nature'. Today, same-sex couples and single people are considered alongside heterosexual couples as prospective adoptive and foster parents. "Attitudes towards same-sex parent families in the UK have changed enormously over a relatively short period of time. In less than half a century we have moved from a situation in which lesbian mothers were ostracised, and gay men were at risk of imprisonment, to a time where same-sex couples can marry, adopt children jointly, and become the joint legal parents of children born through assisted reproductive technologies," says Golombok.

"But it's important to remember that these laws are far from universal.

Lesbian and gay relationships remain a criminal offence in some countries of the world with lesbian and gay people still living in fear of their lives."

Families aren't self-contained units. How do parents handle the prejudice they and their children are almost bound to encounter and how do children cope with what are perceived as 'differences'? Sometimes the attitudes of the wider world make things hard. While children of same-sex parents are just as likely to flourish as those with heterosexual parents, children with lesbian or gay parents have to 'explain' their families in a way that their peers don't. The need to explain can be burdensome.

"It's stigmatisation outside the family, rather than relationships within it, that creates difficulties for children in new family forms," says Golombok.

Children born through egg or sperm donation grow up with a realisation that they have a biological mother or father who may not live with them. The research covered in *Modern Families* shows that the question of disclosure – informing children conceived through donated gametes about their genetic parentage – is a foggy one.

Legislation that took effect in 2005 gives anyone conceived with donated gametes after that date the right to have, at the age of 18, access to information about the identity of their donor via records held by the UK's Human Fertilisation and Embryology Authority (HFEA). Not until 2023 will it begin to be apparent how many donor-conceived young people might seek information about their donors from the HFEA. If adoption law is any guide, the numbers will not be insignificant.

As the legislation stands, young people will not know that they have been donor conceived unless they have been told – and only those with this knowledge will have any reason to seek access to the information held about their donor. This situation puts the onus firmly on the parents to

make the decision about disclosure. Interestingly, although many parents profess the intention of bringing their children up with the knowledge that they were donor conceived, significant numbers of parents never find the right moment to broach the subject.

Golombok says: "Parents fear that telling children about their donor conception will jeopardise the loving relationship that has developed between the child and the non-genetic parent. However, our research has shown this fear to be unfounded. Parents who are open with their children when they are young – before they reach school age – say that their children accept this information and are not distressed by it. Finding out in adolescence or adulthood appears to be more difficult to accept."

Modern Families is a timely reminder that every family is different – and that families are both fluid and flexible. There is more variation within family types than between them. Many of the newer routes helping people to fulfil their desires to have a family are still in their infancy. Progress is never smooth – and, quite rightly, innovations in conception are bound to be, and need to be, a matter for public debate. Research by Golombok and her colleagues, at Cambridge and beyond, provides a firm and informed basis for discourse to take place.

12 March 2015

⇨ The above is reprinted with kind permission from the University of Cambridge. Please visit www.cam. ac.uk for further information.

© 2018 University of Cambridge

Teenage pregnancy rates reach lowest level on record

Teenage pregnancy rates in England and Wales have fallen to their lowest level on record.

In 2015, there were 20,351 conceptions to girls under 18, a 10% decrease from 2014 , according to the Office for National Statistics (ONS).

There were 21 pregnancies out of every 1,000 teenage girls in 2015, compared with 47.1 in 1969 when comparable records began.

In 1969, there were 45,495 teenage pregnancies.

The ONS said there could be a number of factors behind the figures, including a shift in aspirations of young women towards education, a stigma associated with being a teenage mother, better sex education and improved access to contraceptives.

It also named the areas with the highest rates of teenage pregnancy, including Blackpool, Burnley and Kingston upon Hull.

Across all age groups the number of conceptions had risen slightly.

In 2015, the estimated number of conceptions in England and Wales

rose by 0.7% to 876,934, from 871,038 the year before.

The figures also show that most babies are conceived out of wedlock.

The ONS said there has been a long-term rise in the percentage of pregnancies occurring outside marriage or civil partnership, reaching 57% in 2015 in England and Wales.

During 2015, 69% of conceptions outside marriage or civil partnership resulted "in a maternity", compared with 92% of conceptions within marriage or civil partnership.

The ONS said the percentage of abortions varied by age group.

Women aged 30 to 34 had the lowest percentage of abortions in 2015, while girls under 16 had the highest rate at six in ten conceptions.

Overall, 21.2% of conceptions led to abortion, the figures show.

ONS statistician Nicola Haines said: "Under-18 conception rates have declined by 55% since 1998, whilst for women aged 30 and over, conception rates have increased by 34%."

Izzi Seccombe, chairwoman of the Local Government Association's

Community Wellbeing Board, said: "The Government's decision to make sex and relationships education compulsory in schools will help young people to develop healthy relationships, delay early pregnancy, and look after their sexual health.

"However, we are concerned that all this good work could be put at risk by the false economy of government cuts to councils' public health funding, and that the drop in teenage conception rates will be even harder to sustain.

"Getting it right on teenage pregnancy will not only make a difference to individual lives, it will help narrow inequalities and reduce long-term demand on health and social care services."

Professor Kevin Fenton, Director of Health and Wellbeing at Public Health England, said: "It is good news that the rate of teenage pregnancy continues to decline, as it is linked to poor future health for both parents and babies.

"We want to maintain this downward trend and support young people to make informed choices so that they can secure the best possible future for them and their children."

22 March 2017

⇨ The above is reprinted with kind permission from The Press Association. Please visit www.belfasttelegraph.co.uk for further information.

© 2018 The Press Association

How teenage pregnancy collapsed after birth of social media

John Bingham, Social Affairs Editor

Have Facebook and Snapchat helped stop teenagers having sex? New figures show teenage pregnancies plunging to record low since social media explosion.

Teenage pregnancy rates have almost halved since the birth of social media as a global phenomenon, official figures show.

The rate of pregnancies among girls under 18 in England and Wales has dropped by 45 per cent since 2007 and now stands at the lowest level since records began almost 50 years ago, according to the Office for National Statistics.

The startling decrease has prompted a host of theories including sex education classes paying off, changing attitudes to young motherhood and the impact of immigration.

But others have speculated that it could be that young people are simply spending less time physically in each other's company because of social media – a phenomenon which went global around 2007, the year after Facebook expanded beyond university campuses.

The drop in teenage pregnancies has been accompanied by evidence of decreases in other traditionally risky behaviours such as drinking and drug taking.

Children's charities and experts have repeatedly warned that the explosion of social media is exposing young people to new dangers from online bullying to 'sexting' and sexual exploitation by strangers.

But the new figures suggest that the change in how teenagers conduct their social lives could also be helping make them safer.

Overall 22,653 girls under 18 got pregnant in England and Wales in 2014 – a drop of almost seven per cent in a single year. Among under-16s it fell by ten per cent in the same period.

The rate of conceptions among under-18s dropped from 41.6 per 1,000 girls in the age-group in 2007 to 22.9 per 1,000 in 2014.

Professor David Paton, an economist at Nottingham University Business School – who was among the first to suggest a social media effect on pregnancies – said it was striking that a similar pattern is emerging in other countries such as New Zealand.

"It does potentially fit in terms of timing," he said.

"Rather than sitting at bus stops with a bottle of vodka they are doing it remotely with their friends."

Professor David Paton

He argued that better access to contraception could not explain the fall as it coincides with cuts to sexual health services in many areas amid a period of major austerity.

One other possibility, he said, was that major improvements in schools in areas such as London around the same time might have played a part.

But he added: "Nobody really knows why we've got this sudden change around about 2007 to 2008."

Meanwhile the number of pregnancies among older women rose, continuing a long-term trend towards later motherhood.

Notably, the figures also show that 7.8 per cent of pregnancies involving married women ended in an abortion – the highest level for 12 years.

Yet among unmarried women the abortion rate fell slightly from 31.2 per cent of conceptions to 31 per cent.

Clare Murphy, director of external affairs at the abortion provider British Pregnancy Advisory Service (BPAS) said access to contraception and sex education had "undoubtedly" played a part in the declining teenage pregnancy rate but she agreed with Prof Paton's suggestion of a social media effect.

"The plummeting level of teenage drinking, for example, may be reducing the likelihood of unprotected sex, and teenagers are also increasingly socialising online, limiting the opportunities for sexual activity," she said.

She added: "As we have seen decreases in conception rates among the under-25s, the largest rise was for women aged 35–39 (a percentage increase of 2.3 per cent).

"Women are increasingly being chivvied about starting their families in their 20s, but the reality is many will wait until their 30s to do so.

"The reasons for this are diverse and will include the time it takes to obtain financial and career security, and not least finding the right person to embark on parenthood with.

"Rather than chastising women, we should support their choices.

"There may be some increased risks with later motherhood, but these need to be kept well in perspective, and women respected as the best judges of when it is best for them to have children."

9 March 2016

⇨ The above extract is reprinted with kind permission from The Telegraph. Please visit www.telegraph.co.uk for further information.

© Telegraph Media Group Limited 2014

Teenage pregnancy rates drop to record low since 1969, figures show

By Amy Packham

The number of teenage girls getting pregnant in England and Wales is the lowest it has been since 1969.

The rate for girls under 18 becoming mothers was 22.9 conceptions per thousand 15- to 17-year-olds in 2014, the Office for National Statistics (ONS) revealed.

The number of teenage mothers fell to 22,653 in 2014, compared with 24,306 in 2013, a decrease of 6.8%. In 1969, when records started, there were 45,495 teenage pregnancies.

The rate of teen pregnancies has more than halved since 1998, when there were 47 conceptions per thousand teenagers.

Alison Hadley, director of the Teenage Pregnancy Knowledge Exchange at the University of Bedfordshire, led the Teenage Pregnancy Strategy – a long-term project that began in 1999.

Hadley called this finding an "extraordinary achievement".

"Despite the big reduction, the job is not done," she said.

"England continues to lag behind comparable western European countries, teenagers continue to be at greatest risk of unplanned pregnancy and outcomes for some young parents and their children remain disproportionately poor."

The official figures also showed the rate of conception among under-16s was down 10%, with an estimated 4,160 pregnancies in 2014 compared with 4,648 in 2013.

The ONS also revealed variations in pregnancy rates between different areas, ranging from 18.8 (per 1,000 women aged 15 to 17) in the South East and South West to 30.2 in the North East.

Sexual health charity FPA's CEO Natika H. Halil said it is great there has been a continued decrease in the teenage pregnancy rate.

"Not all teenage pregnancies are unplanned or unwanted, but young people who become parents under 18 have a higher risk of poorer health, education, economic and social outcomes," she said.

"This ongoing reduction is the result of a joint effort, including the legacy of the Teenage Pregnancy Strategy, which ended in 2010, and the continued work of health and education professionals to support young people in making informed choices that are best for their lives."

However, Halil said for the areas which have seen continued higher rates since 2013, it is important there is investment in and commitment to prevention services.

"In the last year we have seen the Government fail to make sex and relationships education statutory and significant cuts made to public health budgets in England," she added.

"Neither is going to help bring the country's teenage pregnancy rate more in line with other countries in Europe and both need to be given serious consideration."

10 March 2016

⇨ The above is reprinted with kind permission from *The Huffington Post*. Please visit www. huffingtonpost.co.uk for further information.

© 2018 AOL (UK) Limited

Good progress but more to do

An extract from Public Health England report on Teenage pregnancy and young parents.

Introduction

In many ways, the focus on teenage pregnancy seen in England during the last 15 years or so has been one of the success stories in the public health field.

The conception rate for young women aged 15 to 17 has been halved since 1998 and is now the lowest it has been since recordkeeping began in the late 1960s.

But that doesn't mean the problem has been solved. Far from it. The conception rate still remains higher than a number of other western European countries and the progress made has been uneven across England.

About a third of local authorities have a rate significantly higher than the England average and even in those areas that have low rates, inequalities exist between wards.

These variations matter. Teenage pregnancy is both a cause and consequence of health and education inequalities.

Young parents want to do the best for their children and for many the outcomes are poor.

Teenage mothers are also at higher risk of missing out on further education – a fifth of young women aged 16 to 18 who are not in education, employment or training are teenage mothers. Young fathers are also more likely to have poor education and have a greater risk of being unemployed in adult life.

Their children can be affected too. They have a 25 per cent higher risk of a low birth weight, 44 per cent higher risk of infant mortality, 63 per cent higher risk of experiencing child poverty and at age five are more likely to have developmental delays.

This is the reason why the drive to reduce teenage pregnancy has been coupled with increasing the support available to young mothers and fathers.

Children in poverty – 63 per cent higher risk for children born to women under 20

Rates of adolescents not in education, employment or training (NEET) – 21 per cent of the estimated number of 16–18 female NEETs are teenage mothers

Adult poverty – By age 30, women who were teenage mothers are 22 per cent more likely to be living in poverty than mothers giving birth aged 24 or over. Compared with older fathers, young fathers are twice as likely to be unemployed, even after taking account of deprivation.

Infant mortality rate – 44 per cent higher risk for babies born to women under 20

Neonatal mortality and stillbirth – 30 per cent higher rate of stillbirths to babies born to women under 20

Incidence of low birth weight of term babies – 15 per cent higher risk for babies born to women under 20

Maternal smoking prevalence (including during pregnancy) – Mothers under 20 are twice as likely to smoke before and during pregnancy and three times more likely to smoke throughout pregnancy

Breastfeeding initiation and prevalence at 6–8 weeks – Mothers under 20 are a third less likely to initiate breastfeeding and half as likely to be breastfeeding at 6–8 weeks

Emotional health and well–being – Mothers under 20 experience higher rates of poor mental health for up to three years after the birth

Taken together the twintrack approach helps ensure every child and young person enjoys the best start in life.

The story so far

The focus on teenage pregnancy as a major public health issue began in 1999 with the then government's Teenage Pregnancy Strategy. The strategy called on councils to lead local partnership boards and ringfenced budgets were allocated to help tackle the issue. The ambitious target of halving teenage pregnancy by 2010 was set.

It saw local areas make changes to the way they delivered relationships and sex education in schools, provided access to contraceptive services, involved youth and community practitioners and improved the support available to young parents.

It took time for the Strategy to have an impact on such a complex issue. But after 2008 progress accelerated as the cumulative actions taken by councils and their health partners became embedded in local services. By 2010 there was a 27 per cent drop with the steep downward trend continuing in the following three years. The conception rate has now dropped to half the 1998 level.

However, that overall figure masks what is happening on a local level. Reductions at a council level vary from 30 per cent to 70 per cent, including stark differences between areas with similar demographics; and almost a third of councils have a rate significantly higher than the England average.

Since 2010 the Government has continued to make reducing teenage pregnancy a priority. In 2013, public health transferred from NHSE to local authorities including the 5–19 years services. From October 2015 the commissioning of the 0–5 years services transferred to local authorities, offering the opportunity to focus on integrating work on prevention and support for young parents.

Continuing to reduce the rate of under-18 conceptions is one of the key objectives of the Department of Health Sexual Health Improvement Framework and is also one of the 66 indicators in the 2013 Public Health Outcomes Framework (PHOF).

⇨ The above extract is reprinted with kind permission from Local Government UK. Please visit www.local.gov.uk for further information.

© 2018 Local Government UK

Annual Fatherhood Survey 2016

An extract from a report by The Centre for Social Justice.

The dad gap

This year The Centre for Social Justice has teamed up with public opinion platform, Bheard.com, to conduct a 'Survey of Fatherhood' in the UK. Our exclusive opinion poll conducted by YouGov identifies an alarming 'Dad Gap' in the UK:

⇨ Attendance at parenting and antenatal classes is increasingly a middle class preserve; low-income fathers are half as likely to go to parenting and antenatal classes as higher income fathers: 71% vs 31%.

– The good news for government is that 87% of low-income fathers found parenting and antenatal classes useful, compared to 65% of higher income fathers.

– More needs to be done to help fathers before the birth of their first child; 72% of higher income fathers felt prepared for becoming a father for the first time compared to only 60% of lower income fathers saying they felt prepared.

– When asked whether there was any information or guidance provided for new fathers, 55% of low-income fathers said they were left to "pick it up themselves" vs 29% of higher income fathers.

– Poorer fathers suffer the effects of 'digital exclusion' when it comes to finding information and support online. 45% of fathers in the top two household income brackets use the Internet for information compared to 26% in the bottom two household income brackets

In further evidence that Britain has a long way to go in becoming the most father-friendly nation ever, our poll found:

⇨ 47% of all UK fathers feel their role isn't valued by society and almost half (46%) of the lowest income fathers reported a lack of "good" fatherhood role models.

⇨ New fathers are crying out for better social and emotional support rather than being told to "man up". Nearly three out of five Dads (57%) say they felt emotionally unsupported when they first became a father.

⇨ Only 25% of British Dads feel that there is enough support to help them play a positive role in family life. 78% of Dads say there is less support available to fathers than for mothers.

⇨ A new breed of 'Google Dads' is emerging: Our poll uncovers a dramatic rise in the use of the Internet as a guide to parenting, with a fourfold increase in Internet use since the early noughties.

⇨ New dads now go online for information and advice on being a father. 38% of fathers of under-fives get their information online, compared to 30% who got information from parenting classes.

Attending antenatal or parenting classes

71% of fathers with a household income over £70,000 vs 31% of fathers with a household income under £20,000 attended a parenting or antenatal classes before becoming a father for the first time.

85% of fathers who attended antenatal or parenting classes with a household income below £20,000 said they were "useful" compared to 67% of fathers with a household income over £70,000.

Becoming a dad for the first time

72% of fathers with a household income over £70,000 vs 60% of fathers with a household income under £20,000 felt prepared to be a first-time father.

55% of fathers with household incomes under £20,000 said they didn't approach anyone at all and were left to "pick it up" by themselves compared to 29% of fathers from households with an income over £70,000.

The emergence of Google dads

New dads go online for information and advice on being a father: 38% of fathers of under fives get their information online, compared to 30% of the same fathers who got their information from parenting classes.

Perceptions of fatherhood

47% of all UK fathers feel their role isn't valued by society.

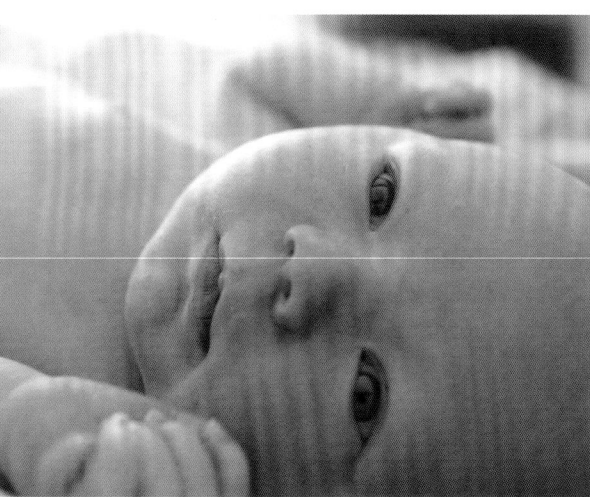

Support for fathers

57% of all UK fathers said there was not much or no emotional support on becoming a father.

78% of all UK fathers feel less support is available for fathers than for mothers.

Being a father is getting harder

54% of all UK fathers think it is difficult to be a father these days.

⇨ The above extract is reprinted with kind permission from The Centre for Social Justice. Please

visit www.centreforsocialjustice.org.uk for further information.

© 2018 The Centre for Social Justice

The myth of the fatherless society

An article from The Conversation.

THE CONVERSATION

Anna Tarrant, Lecturer in Sociology, University of Lincoln and Michael Ward, Senior Lecturer in Applied Social Science, Swansea University

Society has a problem with absent men. Every other week it seems there are warnings that fathers aren't there for their families, and that men are absent from social institutions like childcare, schools and other support settings. It's a problem that is driving concern over how children are being raised, as well as the wider difficulties it can cause outside the family.

This "crisis of fatherlessness" debate has remarkable endurance, attracting regular and considerable public and policy attention, particularly in recent years.

Andy Cook, chief executive of think-tank the Centre for Social Justice (CSJ), recently claimed that almost half of all children born in Britain today will not be living with both of their parents by the time they reach the age of 15. Cook said that parenting is too much of a throwaway culture, adding that "we need a societal shift in perspective from regarding fathers as a dispensable extra to recognising their value as a crucial pillar in a child's life".

The CSJ previously found that 75% of the public believe that fathers not being present is a serious problem. However, referring to the issue as a "crisis" is a massive leap from the CSJ's "serious problem". And using it as a key cause for issues like the poverty and social disadvantage that young people face today is problematic to say the least.

Fathers matter

In a nutshell, the fatherlessness debate focuses on the lack of men in the lives of their children – particularly boys. Fathers certainly matter to children whether they are absent or present; however, it is when dads are confidently engaged in the lives of their children that there is a positive effect on child well-being and family relationships.

But the 'fear' is overblown. The blame for young people's poverty or any other issues are firmly rooted in assumptions about the failures of parents: working-class fathers in particular are stigmatised, branded with lazy stereotypes like 'deadbeat dads' and 'feckless fathers'.

Though it makes sense to worry that dads aren't present, it is not so easy to say that the behaviour of the stereotypes are the sole cause of young people's problems generally. Rarely, if ever, does the discussion include professional men whose busy lives might mean they miss out on spending time with their children, or whose children are schooled away from home. It also says a lot about how we feel about single, female-headed households.

Present without presence

So where is this concern coming from? Look at the census data between 2005 and 2012 and it shows that – despite increased attention to fatherless families – the proportion of lone parent families with dependent children in the UK has gone up only marginally since the early 2000s.

The data also ignores the range of social fathering that takes place more and more in reconstituted families. So while the number of single parents has stayed consistent, they may have met new partners. And even where parents remain alone, parenting can occur across households, as well as within.

Both men and women from different generations in the family can also play an important part in raising and supporting children where the father is not present, either informally or as kinship carers, although this is often with limited financial support.

Looking to the young men themselves, the social problems they face are often reduced to gender just to make them easier for the public to understand. This is no help when, for example, both men and women can experience things like poverty, and it shouldn't be assumed that only men can help men. Fathers and other male role models certainly do play an important part in helping young men to flourish, but women and men in other mentoring positions can provide the care, trust and support that young men might need.

Young fathers

Research has previously found that fatherhood can have as much of an effect on the health of men – particularly young men – as it does on women. While we are finding that fatherhood matters to young men and they do desire to be there for their children, they are often considered more of a risk by professionals – through severe material disadvantage or criminality – to themselves or their children.

Young dads with extensive support needs require practical help with education, training, employment, housing and finance, and so are often overlooked as capable carers – simply because they are not recognised as being as caring as women. If support services were more father inclusive and attentive to the diverse needs of fathers from all walks of life, this could help them more effectively to be involved in raising their children.

The research doesn't back up the 'crisis', and is in fact looking at the wrong issue. Fathers still need support, but they cannot be blamed for all the problems their children may face. The way we talk about and address modern families needs to change too. Rather than stigmatising those who do not live as a nuclear family, we would be better off supporting and including them in our changing society.

20 February 2017

⇨ The above is reprinted with kind permission from *The Conversation*. Please visit www.theconversation. com for further information.

© 2010-2018 The Conversation Trust (UK)

Acas publishes new advice to help working dads spend more time with their family

Workplace experts Acas have published a new flexible working guide and top tips on Father's Day to help working dads consider the options available to spend more time with the family whilst working.

From flexi-time to compressed hours, there are multiple ways for fathers to strike a better balance between work and quality family time. Acas' work-life balance guide highlights the full range of options available to dads that are hands-on – both in business and at home.

Acas Head of Information and Guidance, Stewart Gee said:

"Some dads may feel that being a full-time worker means sacrificing spending some quality time with the kids but there are many workplace options out there that they may not be aware of.

"Our new guide could help thousands of dads from missing out on bed times, school plays, parents' evenings and more. The right working pattern can really make a huge difference to family life without affecting business needs.

"As workplace experts, we want to make sure that employers and employees understand the variety of working patterns that are out there because this really can benefit the business as well as the employee."

To celebrate Father's Day, Acas has produced a set of top tips for working dads that could help them get a better work-life balance:

Consider the options: There are a wide range of flexible working arrangements that are available. For example they can cover the way your working hours are organised during the day, such as flexitime that allows you to build up additional time off on occasions when you work late – so you have the option to get in at non-set times to help with school runs. Or you might want to consider job sharing which would mean working less days. Homeworking is also another option. You should properly consider the range of flexible options available and think about what is right for you, your job, and your family.

Speak to your partner: Talk to your partner before speaking to your employer. There are many different combinations that are possible with flexible working to get a better work-life balance and you will need to make sure they fit around your life and work for you as a couple. You may want to work more flexibly when your children are younger, for childcare purposes

or do compressed hours so you get an additional day off but work longer hours on the days you are working - the choice is yours.

Be prepared and think about how it can work for your team/employer: You should prepare for your conversation with your employer by thinking about the practical ways that a flexible working arrangement can work for you, your team and your employer without affecting business or productivity. Showing that you can demonstrate this to your employer will help to show that you have thought about this properly and practically. It is also important to bear in mind that not all flexible working arrangements will be suitable in all workplaces.

Speak to your employer: a good conversation with your employer can allow you both to come up with a good arrangement that works for both of you. For example, options for customer facing roles can be limited but flexi-time, part-time working and job sharing could still be considered. You might find mobile working suitable, which allows an employee to work all or part of their working week at a location away from their employer's workplace. Traditional mobile workers include sales representatives and delivery drivers. See flexible working code and guidance at *The right to request flexible working*.

Look into shared parental leave if you and your partner are both working and expecting a new arrival to the family: If you are going to be a new dad then you might want to think about shared parental leave where couples can share the first year off with the baby. You can check to make sure that you are eligible with this online calculator GOV.UK – Calculate your leave and pay when you have a child.

Stewart Gee added:

"A good balance between an employee's work commitments and family responsibilities can help to reduce stress, absence and increase productivity.

"Of course, flexible working isn't just for parents; employees who have a better work-life balance often have a greater sense of responsibility, ownership and control of their working life. If an employer helps an employee to balance their work and home life this can be rewarded by increased loyalty and commitment."

The right to request flexible working was extended to all employees in April 2014 and is designed to give employers confidence in responding positively to requests and changing workplace cultures for the better. The full guide: Flexible working and work life balance is available from *The right to request flexible working*.

21 June 2015

⇨ The above is reprinted with kind permission from Acas. Please visit www.acas.org.uk for further information.

© 2018 The Advisory, Conciliation and Arbitration Service

Why fathers can't be more involved parents

By Kevin Shafer

In most families, mothers and fathers both work hard. Pew Research recently reported that mums and dads in the US work essentially equal hours when paid work hours are combined with household chores and child care hours.

Pew also reports that fathers are putting more time into their families than ever before. Yet, many social scientists argue that subtle forms of parenting inequality endure. Some scholars and commentators argue that this inequality results from a patriarchal gender ideology: a power dynamic that affects how parents socialise their children and what roles men and women take on in families.

As a scholar who focuses on fathering and men's health, I see my research paint a more complicated picture. While traditional gender attitudes and expectations tell an important part of the story, inequalities between mums and dads are not driven solely by beliefs or interpersonal interactions.

Fathers repeatedly tell researchers they want to be more involved parents, yet public policy and social institutions often prevent them from being the dads they want to be – hurting mums, dads and children alike.

Wasting the 'magic moment'

Engaging dads in prenatal care is a potentially powerful way to help set dads on positive parenting trajectories. I recently participated in a symposium of social work researchers that highlighted the importance of engaging fathers during this 'magic moment' in their lives.

Dads who are actively included in prenatal care form a stronger 'father' identity for themselves and are good parents by virtually any measure. In fact, the impact of the prenatal period is often stronger for dads who are already at risk of having low levels of engagement.

Yet, dads are often actively excluded from prenatal care. Obstetricians' offices are rarely designed in ways that help doctors and nurses engage dads with their unborn child. For example, many ultrasound rooms do not include space for fathers to see their child for the first time. In general, obstetricians emphasise mother and child health – to the exclusion of other members of the family system.

Childbirth courses, similarly, often tell dads they should be supportive, but do little else to address the father's role.

After the baby is born

Family health and well-being are important after babies are born, too. Fathers, like mothers, can experience postpartum depression and struggle with the transition to parenthood. Recently, pediatricians have taken a more substantive role in addressing postpartum depression in mothers. Fathers seldom get the same attention.

This lack of support from the medical profession may hurt families in the long run. My research suggests that being a parent has similar negative effects on the mental health of mothers and fathers. In fact, in some cases, we found that fathers were more likely to experience depression than mothers.

Failing to acknowledge the mental health of fathers can be problematic. Like depression in mothers, paternal depression has negative effects in early childhood and beyond.

Why the workplace may matter the most

Obstacles to more involved fathering extend beyond health care. Many mothers and fathers struggle to balance family and careers. Public and private policies often contribute to the difficulty, forcing parents to prioritise one or the other.

The US is the only industrialised nation in the world that doesn't guarantee paid maternity leave. To make matters worse, few families have a choice as to whether the mother or father stays home: Less than one-fifth of American employers offer paid paternity leave. Meanwhile, several European countries (including France and the UK) have mandated paternity leave.

Research has shown that generous family leave policies positively impact family health, parents' well-being and gender equity in the workplace.

Yet, these benefits may not be enough. For example, many men do not use leave or flexitime if they believe it will damage their careers or reputation. My own research – with colleagues from Brigham Young University – focuses on workplace culture and its significance for fathers. Using data collected from fathers of children aged two to 17, we found that even reluctant fathers were more nurturing, emotionally engaged and better co-parents if they worked for organisations with cultures and policies that promoted family involvement.

Structural barriers hurt all family members

Fathers, like mothers, can help their children grow and learn. It's clear that children in families with fathers benefit from having an engaged, warm, nurturing dad. Likewise, mums, both at home and at work, benefit from dads who share the burden in taking care of children.

The failure to provide explicit, consistent and strong supports for fathers is a failure to pave the way for a more equitable kind of parenting. My research – and that of many others – shows that if fathers are to take on more caregiving at home, they should be provided with the tools to become more engaged with their

families. This would not only distribute parental expectations more evenly, but also eliminate the overly restrictive gender boundaries that limit men and marginalise women.

Yes, I applaud changes that have helped fathers be more involved parents than ever before. But it's not enough. We need cultural and political change that emphasises the significance of fathers for families and the crucial role women play in the workplace.

17 June 2017

⇨ The above is reprinted with kind permission from the *International Business Times*. Source: <u>IBTIMES</u> http://www.ibtimes.com/why-fathers-cant-be-more-involved-parents-2553394 Please visit www.ibtimes.com for further information.

© 2018 International Business Times

The understated affection of fathers

***An article from* The Conversation.** THE C*O*NVERSATION

By Kory Floyd, Proffesor of Communication, University of Arizona

Men may not be from Mars, but – compared to women – they do communicate in very different ways.

Perhaps nowhere is this more evident than in the relationships of fathers and sons. Outwardly, many father and son pairs may appear distant and disengaged. A guy who wouldn't think twice about hugging and kissing his mum might offer his father only a stilted handshake. Dads who shower their daughters with affection may go years without telling their sons they love them. Men are often chided by their wives or mothers for not being willing to show more affection to their dads or their sons.

Such criticisms overlook a larger truth, one that I've spent years exploring as a communication researcher: often for men, showing affection is more about what they do than what they say. Their ways of communicating love can be subtle. And while to outside observers they may seem like weak substitutes for genuine affection, to many fathers and sons they're every bit as meaningful as words, kisses and hugs.

Different ways of expressing love

Glenn, a 41-year-old participant in one of my studies, has what many people would call a typical relationship with his dad, R.J. On Sundays, Glenn and his wife often visit Glenn's parents. While Glenn's wife catches up with her mother-in-law, Glenn and R.J. watch television, tinker with R.J.'s car or tackle a household repair, barely saying a few dozen words to each other over the course of an hour.

In many relationships, these behaviours seem cold or distant. But in the case of Glenn and R.J., the two simply favour actions over words.

My research on affectionate behaviour has consistently shown that, in general, men are more likely to communicate affection by doing something supportive than by making verbal expressions, such as saying or writing "I love you".

While I've found that this is especially true in their relationships with other men, it's also true in their relationships with women. With his guy friends, a typical man is more likely to show his affection by organising a road trip or helping with a roof repair than by saying

"I care about you". Around his wife or mother, he may be more inclined to help with a task that needs doing – mowing the lawn or rotating the tyres on the car – than sending a Hallmark card.

It's easy to devalue these types of behaviors as substitutes for "real" affection. For example, Glenn's wife believes that Glenn and his father prioritise shared activities because they don't know how to express the way they feel about each other.

However, Glenn and his dad say that their favourite, most meaningful times together are spent sharing an activity or working on a specific task. To them, that is the expression of love: it signifies and reinforces how they feel about each other.

The tension between intimacy and masculinity

It's easy to understand why many dads and sons appear indifferent to each other. At least in our culture, affection is commonly communicated through verbal expressions and also through nonverbal gestures such as hugging.

Both of these are less common in relationships between men, making it seem as though there's something missing. But what's really at play is a misunderstanding about the complexity of father-son relationships.

Family communication scholar Mark Morman and I have found that the father and son pair is complicated by the need to negotiate a complex tension between masculinity and intimacy.

On one hand, the bond between dads and sons is a family relationship. People tend to feel closer and more invested in their families than they do in many other social bonds.

On the other hand, the father and son pair is a relationship between two males – one that's

subject to cultural expectations about how men are supposed to act towards each other. Traditional masculinity has tended to privilege qualities like competition, independence and self-sufficiency. This comes at the expense of outward expressions of intimacy, which can convey vulnerability.

Wishing for more

Glenn told me that his dad became less outwardly affectionate towards him once Glenn became a teenager. I've found this evolution in the father and son relationship is quite common. At a certain point, many dads and sons will base their relationships on shared activities instead of shared words. Meanwhile, fathers tend not to curtail verbal displays of affection with their daughters in the same way, nor do mothers with their sons or daughters.

Like Glenn's wife and mother, many women wonder aloud why the men in their lives aren't more expressive and open. From time to time, even Glenn wished aloud that he and his dad could talk about their feelings for each other more directly.

As I explain in my book *The Loneliness Cure*, there's nothing wrong with wanting a more expressive relationship. Indeed, many men do successfully become more verbally affectionate with their fathers or their sons.

There's an important lesson here, though: many male relationships are already richer and more meaningful than they appear to be. And the unique way men relate to one another deserves to be honoured rather than belittled.

13 June 2017

⇨ The above is reprinted with kind permission from *The Conversation*. Please visit www.theconversation.com for further information.

© 2010-2018 The Conversation Trust (UK)

Key facts

⇨ In 2016, there were 4.8 million married (opposite and same sex) or civil partner couple families with dependent children in the UK. There were 1.3 million cohabiting couples with dependent children and 1.9 million single parent families with dependent children. Women accounted for 86 per cent of single parents with dependent children and men the remaining 14 per cent (page 1)

⇨ Of the 13.9 million dependent children living in families, the majority (63 per cent) of dependent children live in a married couple family. The percentage of dependent children living in cohabiting families increased from seven per cent to 15 per cent between 1996 and 2016, while the percentage of dependent children living in single parent families changed little. Married couples with dependent children have more children on average than other family types. In 2016, 55 per cent of single parents with dependent children had one child, whereas 39 per cent of married couples with dependent children had one child (page 1)

⇨ Dual-earner households are now the norm in the UK: in 2014 in more than 68 per cent of couple families both parents were working. Among couple families, the percentage of both parents working full time increased from 26 per cent in 2001 to 31 per cent in 2013 (page 1)

⇨ In 2014, 65 per cent of single parents with one or two dependent children were working compared with 47 per cent of single parents with three or more dependent children. Couple parents with young children (aged under five) were almost twice (78.6 per cent) as likely to be in employment as single parents with young children (40.9 per cent) (page 1)

⇨ The proportion of mothers with children aged between three and four who are in employment increased by almost ten percentage points over the past two decades. In England there are now around 133,000 more mothers, whose youngest child is a toddler, in employment in 2017 (65.1%), compared with 1997 (55.8%). This was largely driven by an increase in full-time employment (page 3)

⇨ Workers in the UK once had the longest week in the EU, but a decline since 2001 in average working hours among fathers means this is no longer the case. In 2001, fathers in the UK worked an average of 46.1 hours per week. By 2013, this had decreased to 43 hours (including part-time workers) (page 5)

⇨ The average working week for all British mothers, including those who work part-time, has increased from 26.8 to 29.1 hours in the same time period (page 5)

⇨ Currently UK fathers are eligible to take one or two weeks paid leave any time within 56 days of the birth (page 11)

⇨ 37% of working families would be unable to cover their housing costs for more than a month if one partner lost their job (page 12)

⇨ Children who eat a main meal at a regular time, rather than snack throughout the day, have healthier diets (page 15)

⇨ Eating the same food as parents is linked to better dietary quality in children. This may be because 'child-friendly' alternatives to adult food are likely to be nutritionally inferior (page 15)

⇨ In families where mothers describe mealtimes as enjoyable or as opportunities to talk, children are less likely to have poorer diets (page 15)

⇨ A recent survey of children aged eight to 12 found that indoor play is now the norm, a third have never splashed in a puddle and the distance children are allowed to play from home has shrunk by 90% since 1970 (page 19)

⇨ Globally, 52 countries have made the physical punishment of children illegal. Sweden was the first in 1979 and France the most recent country with its ban in 2017. The Republic of Ireland banned smacking in 2015 (page 22)

⇨ In Europe, only four countries – Italy, Switzerland, the Czech Republic and the UK – continue to allow the 'reasonable punishment' of children (page 22)

⇨ Around 150,000 English children are growing up in a home with relatives other than their parents (page 24)

⇨ Between 2001 and 2011 the number of children looked after by family members other than parents rose by seven per cent, far exceeding the two per cent growth in the child population as a whole (page 24)

⇨ Up to 3 million children risk going hungry during the school holidays, leaving them vulnerable to malnutrition and undermining their education and life chances (page 25)

⇨ Today 'non-traditional' families outnumber nuclear families in the UK and many other countries (page 22)

⇨ The conception rate for young women aged 15 to 17 has been halved since 1998 and is now the lowest it has been since recordkeeping began in the late 1960s (page 33)

⇨ Attendance at parenting and antenatal classes is increasingly a middle class preserve; low-income fathers are half as likely to go to a parenting and antenatal classes as higher income fathers: 71% vs 31% (page 34)

⇨ New fathers are crying out for better social and emotional support rather than being told to "man up". Nearly three out of five dads (57%) say they felt emotionally unsupported when they first became a father (page 34)

⇨ New dads now go online for information and advice on being a father. 38% of fathers of under-fives get their information online, compared to 30% who got information from parenting classes (page 34)

Child maintenance

Usually paid by the parent who is not the primary caregiver/ day-to-day carer of the child. Designed to provide financial help towards a child's everyday living costs. This can be organised through the Child Maintenance Service, but can also be agreed privately.

Child poverty

In order to live above the poverty line, a family with two adults and two children in the UK needs £349 each week to cover food, transport, shoes, clothes, activities, electricity, gas, water, telephone bills, etc.

Co-habitation

People in an intimate relationship who live together. In the eyes of the law, cohabiting couples do not have the same rights as married couples (for example, a couple who are cohabiting do not qualify to be each others' next of kin).

Co-habiting couple

Two people who live together as a couple but are not married or in a civil partnership. Current trends suggest more couples are choosing to have children in cohabiting rather than married relationships.

Dependent children

Usually defined as persons aged under 16, or 16 to 18 and in full-time education, who are part of a family unit and living in the household.

Family

A domestic group related by blood, marriage or other familial ties living together in a household. A 'traditional' or nuclear family usually refers to one in which a married heterosexual couple raise their biological children together; however, changing family structures has resulted in so-called 'non-traditional' family groups including step-families, families with adopted or foster children, single-parent families and children being raised by same-sex parents.

Lone/single parent

Someone who is raising a child alone, either due to divorce/ separation, widowhood, an absent parent or due to single adoption. The majority of lone parents are women.

Parental responsibility

When an adult has the legal right to take responsibility for the care and well-being of their child(ren) and can make important decisions about things such as food, clothing and education, this is referred to as parental responsibility. Married couples having children together automatically have this right, as do all mothers, but if the parents are unmarried the father only has parental responsibility if certain conditions are met.

Assignments

Brainstorming

⇨ What does the term 'family' mean?

⇨ What types of family units are there?

⇨ What is paternity leave?

⇨ What is a kinship carer?

Research

⇨ Do some research into working families in the UK. Pick another country and compare the number of hours per week parents in each country spend working in comparison to each other. Prepare a graph to show your findings.

⇨ Talk to friends and relatives. How many mothers with young children do they know who work. Ask at least five questions on this subject. Write a short report on your findings and share the results with the rest of your class.

⇨ In pairs, research poverty amongst working families in the UK. Why does poverty exist when people are working and what are the causes? How might this issue be addressed. Write a report on your findings.

⇨ How many of your friends and classmates have a family meal each day? You should prepare a questionnaire about this and ask your classmates to fill it in. When you have gathered your findings, prepare a graph.

⇨ In small groups do some online research into 'kinship carers'. What percentage of children in the UK are brought up by people other than their own parents? When you have gathered your results, create a table to show your findings and share with your class.

Design

⇨ Design a poster aimed at discouraging parents from smacking their children.

⇨ Produce a six-page cookery book which gives quick, nutritious recipes to encourage working parents with little time to provide healthy meals for their children.

⇨ Design an illustration to highlight the key points of the article shown on page 17.

⇨ Look at the infogram on page 27. Design your own infogram using the data shown.

Oral

⇨ As a class, discuss whether you think the Government is doing enough to help working parents who are struggling to make ends meet. What could they do to help these families?

⇨ In pairs, go through this book and discuss the cartoons you come across. Think about what the artists were trying to portray with each illustration.

⇨ In pairs, stage a discussion between two parents where one of you is trying to persuade the other that it is wrong to smack a child. You should take it in turns to play the role of the persuader.

⇨ As a class, discuss why you think teenage pregnancy rates are continuing to drop. What more do you think could be done to reduce the rates of pregnancy in the under-18s.

Reading/writing

⇨ Write a one-paragraph definition of poverty.

⇨ Write a one-paragraph definition of parental leave.

⇨ Read the article on page 3 and write a blog explaining why you think more mothers with young children are working full-time.

⇨ Imagine you are a new father and your working hours are long. You wish you could spend more time with your new baby. Write a letter to your employer explaining how you feel and asking if you can reduce your hours slightly in the short-term.

⇨ The article on page 28 says "families come in many guises". Write an essay giving your views on the different types of family units which exist in the present day. Do you think that children growing up in same-sex households will thrive any differently to children growing up in a nuclear family. You should write at least two A4 pages explaining the reasons you feel the way you do.

⇨ In small groups discuss whether you feel it is right for mothers with young children to work. What are the reasons they work? Do they choose to or maybe they have to. Make notes on your discussion and feedback to your class.

⇨ Imagine you are an agony aunt/uncle. A boy of ten has written to you saying his parents are both working and too busy to spend time with him. He is given plenty of money and bought anything he wants. But what he really wants is their time. Write a suitable reply. Give him advice on how he might broach the subject with his parents.

Acknowledgements

The publisher is grateful for permission to reproduce the material in this book. While every care has been taken to trace and acknowledge copyright, the publisher tenders its apology for any accidental infringement or where copyright has proved untraceable. The publisher would be pleased to come to a suitable arrangement in any such case with the rightful owner.

Images

All images courtesy of iStock except pages 8 and 10, Vectors: 11, 23, 24, 31, and 38 Morguefile: pages 13, 14, 18 and 29 Pixabay: page 39 freepik.

Illustrations

Don Hatcher: pages 1 & 20. Simon Kneebone: pages 17 & 36. Angelo Madrid: pages 9 & 32.

Additional acknowledgements

With thanks to the Independence team: Shelley Baldry, Sandra Dennis, Jackie Staines and Jan Sunderland.

Tina Brand

Cambridge, January 2018